The
Speckled Brook Trout

EDITED AND ILLUSTRATED
BY LOUIS RHEAD

THE DERRYDALE PRESS

LANHAM AND NEW YORK

THE DERRYDALE PRESS

Published in the United States of America
by The Derrydale Press
4720 Boston Way, Lanham, Maryland 20706

Distributed by NATIONAL BOOK NETWORK, INC.

Originally published by R. H. Russell 1902
First Derrydale paperback printing with french folds 2000

ISBN 1-56833-157-6 (alk. paper)

The paper used in this publication meets the minimum requirements of
American National Standard for Information Sciences—Permanence of
Paper for Printed Library Materials, ANSI/NISO Z39.48-1992.
Manufactured in the United States of America.

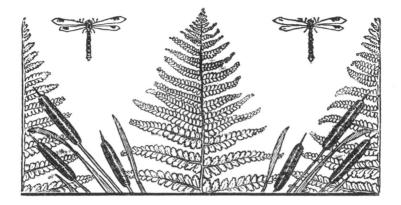

PREFACE

THE extreme popularity of the Brook Trout
has been fully proved by the host of anglers
who fish for him, and it can scarcely be necessary to solicit their favor toward a volume embellished with pictures reproduced in later and
better methods than any that have hitherto appeared,
and with contributions by different experts well known
in departments of the art of angling.

The Editor originally intended to issue a series of
volumes under the title of "A Library of Rod and
Gun," and still may do so should a kindly reception be
given this volume by lovers of nature and of angling.

The first object of this work is to supply general
information on the *Salvelinus fontinalis*. It is hoped
that it will also prove of interest to amateurs as well as
to expert anglers, who will add it to their list of books
to take on their trips to read and re-read at odd times—

E

not too bulky or crowded with technical terms or matter of little interest to the average fisherman who is interested in angling only as a sport or pleasure and change from the activity of city life and business cares.

So much has been written and still remains to be written, an Editor's greatest difficulty is to condense matter pertaining to this particular fish when articles are contributed by a number of writers, but, for the generous assistance (in many small details) of two veteran editor-authors, Charles Hallock and Wm. C. Harris, who have for more than half a century cast the fly and used the pen, the Editor's incompetency would have been more apparent.

My thanks are due to Mr. Annin for his article on " Winged Enemies of Trout; " again to Mr. Hallock for his delightful poem; and to the memory of the late Nelson Cheney, who but a short time before his sudden death cheerfully gave me permission to use, and promised to add matter to his article on " Trout Propagation " from the State report; to Mrs. Mary Orvis Marbury for her selection and arrangement of the colored sheet of flies, made especially by her for this volume; indeed, to all the authors who have contributed their best efforts and whose friendly interest made the labor most agreeable, and lastly to Mr. Russell, who has in every way been lavish, not only in expenditure but in many little artistic details which have made all his books so choice.

PREFACE

In behalf of the Publisher, I wish to acknowledge indebtedness to the courtesy of Harper & Brothers for the use of an article written thirty years ago by Charles Hallock in " The Fishing Tourist," and to *Town Topics* for the use of parts of an article on the old and the changed Adirondacks.

LOUIS RHEAD.

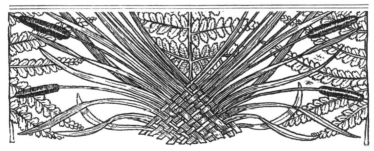

G

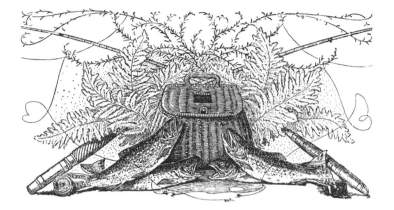

CONTENTS

I

CONTENTS

J

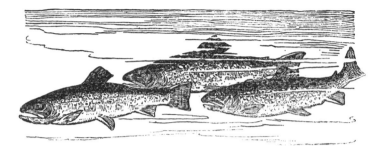

ILLUSTRATIONS

K

BAPTISM OF THE BROOK TROUT.

I AM Salmo Fontinalis,
  To the sparkling fountain born,
And my home is where oxalis,
  Heather bell and rose adorn
    The crystal basin in the dell,
    (Undine the wood-nymph knows it well,)
    That is where I love to dwell.

There was I baptized and christened,
  'Neath the sombre aisles of oak,
Mute the cascade paused and listened,
  Never a word the brooklet spoke;
    Bobolink was witness then,
    Likewise Ousel, Linnet, Wren,
    And all the brownies joined "amen."

Noted oft in ancient story,
  Erst from immemorial time,
Poets, anglers, hermits hoary
  Confirm my vested rights sublime.
    All along the mountain range,
    " 'Tis writ in mystic symbols strange :
    " Naught shall abrogate or change."

Thus as Salmo Fontinalis
  Recognized the wide world o'er,*
In my limpid crystal palace,
  Content withal, I ask no more ;
    Leaping through the rainbow spray,
    Snatching flies the livelong day.
    Naught to do but live and play.

* But scientists have changed this most appropriate designation to
S. Salvelinus, more's the pity !

GENERAL DESCRIPTION OF THE TROUT FAMILY

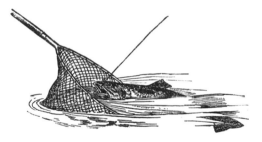

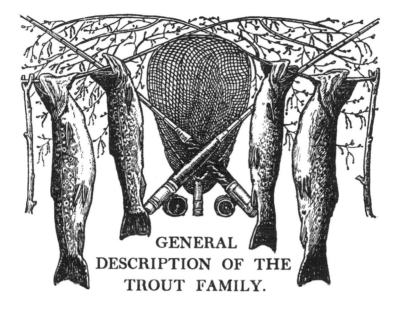

GENERAL DESCRIPTION OF THE TROUT FAMILY.

As Old as the Hills.

ACCORDING to Dr. Shufeldt, an eminent and trustworthy authority, the Salmonidæ date back to the Tertiary Period. He thinks it probable that at the opening of the Glacial Epoch the fresh waters of North America swarmed with various Salmonoid fishes. At the close of that epoch, all the streams and basins which had been subjected to its influence were gouged out and destroyed, and their ichthyic tenants summarily dispossessed. One direct result was to drive a portion into the sea, notably the salmons and the sea trout, which there became habilitated.

The effect of the ice-blanket which so long over-laid the earth was to cool the earth's heated and plastic crust, thereby causing shrinkage, which in turn created fissures, both superficial and subterrene; and these served as conduits for the fluvial output from the dis-solving glacial sheet, and as passageways for the salmonidæ.

Distribution.

Throughout subsequent ages subterranean streams have played a very important part in fish distribution, especially in affording passage under mountain eleva-tions and high table-lands, which would otherwise have proved insurmountable obstacles to superficial transit. Of the existence of a subterranean fluvial system co-extensive with the continental area, and having intimate connection with the ocean, we have abundant manifestations. The remarkable fresh-water ebullitions in the Gulf of Mexico, the fathomless sink-holes and mammoth springs in the adjacent peninsula of Florida, the re-entering "zanates" on the coast of Mexico, and the copious gushes of oil, gas, and water which break out of the sands and rocks all over the continent, are striking and familiar attestations. So, also, sudden changes are occasionally observed in the quality and color of interior ponds, with metamor-phoses of their bottom floors, and of the living organisms which they generate and nurture; and there are intermittent ebbs and flows in the Great Lakes, after the similitude of tides. Many lakes do not diminish by outflow, evaporation, or absorption, in the hottest weather, nor overflow in the wettest seasons, remaining always at a uniform stage. Others suddenly lose half their volume, or drain off altogether. Some swarm with fish at times, and again are apparently barren. All of these phenomena are easily accounted for on the hypothesis of underground connection and in no other way.

As a matter of fact, there is a far more copious and extensive fluvial system under the earth than there is on top of it, any engorgement thereof forcing the flow to the surface, where it finds vent and manifestation through crater cones, geysers, sink-holes, artesian wells, and intermittent springs; also throwing out fish, not eyeless cave-dwellers, but wide-awake, lusty and well-formed specimens of whitefish, sunfish, goggle-eyes, mud-cats, blue-cats, suckers, eels, bass, and pike-perch, as well as lizards and sea-shrimps. We do not find trout represented in the list because it is a primitive species, the subterranean streams having accomplished their general distribution ages ago, under the dispensation of the period. Blind fishes are not thrown out, because they are committed to the lock-up for life, segregated in underground pockets which have, perhaps, no available outlets. At all events, the eyeless fishes which we find in the Mammoth Cave of Ken-

3

tucky and elsewhere, have become so adapted to their
environment and to acquired methods of procuring
subsistence, that they seem content and attempt no
exit. It is not assumed that the hard lethe-like waters
of the deeper fluvial veins take any part in this economy of fish distribution, for assuredly no life can exist
therein, impregnated as they are with salts and base
solutions. Surface water, too, imbibes the impurities
of the earth or soil over which it passes, and it is only
when it has been filtered by percolation through sand
and gravel beds that it becomes as pure as when it
first descended in rainfall. In such pellucid fluid,
drawn fresh from the bosom of mother earth, the trout
thrive best, and in its vivifying arteries, borne underground, the salmonidæ have been passed from one
antipodal locality to another, at various depths, according to the lay of the land.

Distribution by other than subterranean waterways
is various. The presence of alien species in landlocked
waters is often due to overflows, freshets, and cata-
clysms. Transportation by migratory birds and even
by insects, and precipitation by cloud-bursts and water-
spouts, are of frequent occurrence. There is beyond
all an accepted theory of aerial incubation of fish ova
which are held in suspension in the upper atmosphere
until the hatched-out fry drop to earth or convenient
water spaces in some rainfall. One most potential
factor in mechanical distribution is the sturdy pelican,
whose range of habitat is of great extent, reaching

The Willowemoc.

from the Gulf of Mexico to the sub-Arctic regions. In his capacious pouch he will carry quantities of assorted fish, alive, over long distances, often sitting down beside some lake or pond to feed upon his catch, and spilling the overplus into the water.

In current years, human agency is scattering broadcast, populating new streams or rehabilitating those which have become barren. Indeed, the presence of trout in a large majority of amorphous locations can be historically accounted for. For instance, *s. fontinalis*, which is now diffused all over the Appalachian Ridge in Virginia, Tennessee, North and South Carolina, and even in Northeastern Georgia, often attaining a weight of two pounds, was introduced by General Wade Hampton some fifty years ago, and only last summer I saw him at Sapphire, at the age of eighty-seven, enjoying the fruits of his providential forethought. The speckled trout of Castalia, O., were planted by the club which appropriated that famous spring and converted it into a fruitful stream a quarter of a century back. The monster rainbow trout (*s. iridius*), of Macon County, N. C., were planted at Highlands twenty years ago by Henry Stewart, of New Jersey, and the Sapphire Lake trout, of the same species, by the Toxaway Company, who are chiefly Pittsburg gentlemen. Some of these introduced rainbow trout have been caught weighing five pounds, and even more. The rainbow trout of Cumberland County, in central North Carolina, were planted at my request by

D. C. Ravenel, of the United States Fish Commission. German trout (*s. fario*) and Loch Leven trout (*s. levenensis*) have been introduced from abroad into many locations never before occupied by any of the Salmo family, and are found to thrive. In fine, the brook trout of North America and his congeners, large and small, not only " use " in mountain-streams, but in the wide rivers and lakes, as well as in salty estuaries, and along the sea-shores. They occupy the whole of British America except the continental midway and are included in no less than thirty-nine States and Territories. Trout of some sort are found in the six New England States, New York, New Jersey, Pennsylvania, Maryland, Virginia, West Virginia, North Carolina, South Carolina, Georgia, Tennessee, Kentucky, *Ohio, Indiana*, Michigan, Wisconsin, Minnesota, Iowa, *Missouri, Arkansas*, New Mexico, Colorado, *Nebraska, South Dakota, North Dakota*, Montana, Wyoming, Idaho, Washington, Oregon, California, Arizona, Chihuahua, Texas, and Alaska. It is not native to any of those italicized, and is found in very limited portions only of New Jersey, Maryland, South Carolina, Georgia, Tennessee, Kentucky, and Texas. Since a century ago we have discovered and enumerated the most of them and, at last, *dios gratios!* affixed a nomenclature (more or less trinomial) which it may be hoped will stand as long as men fish and trout swim; or at least during the lifetime of the present generation.

6

Species and Varieties.

In making these traverses from one geographical division to another, and from one quality of water to another, as affected by impregnation of salts, oxides, and what not, the trout creation must have undergone those physical modifications and changes in habits, and perhaps in markings and coloration, which are conspicuous throughout the family; thereby establishing from time to time new species, as well as varieties not recognized by scientists as species. These find taxonomic expression in kaleidoscopic body-patterns (like the orchids and begonias), as well as in form, size, weight, tint of flesh, and rapidity of growth. Thus we have the diminutive blue-back of the Rangeleys, seldom exceeding four ounces in average weight; the gigantic lake trout (*namaycush*), attaining 100 pounds; the sea trout of British America, a purely marine fish, ranging coastwise from Maine to Alaska, feeding along shore, spawning in the estuaries at the head of the tide, and seldom running up more than a mile or two into the fresh-water streams; the red-spotted Dolly Vardens of California; the rainbow trout of the Rockies; the red trout of Idaho; the black-spotted varieties of the Continental Divide; the steelheads of Oregon; the olivaceous trouts of our Eastern lakes; the black togue of Maine; the silvery trout of the Penobscot Basin; the white trout of Loch Lomond in the Province of New Brunswick; and, best

7

known and most attractive of all, the radiant brook
trout of New England, with its spangles of crimson,
blue, and orange, its mottled upper fins and vermiculated back, its crimson pectoral fins edged with black
and white, its varying weights, its gameness on the
hook and off it, its bravery in the ring, and its all-round
vigor and beauty—all of which give to it an individu-
ality which has made it conspicuous in song and story
since the day of its advent. The Messenger Brothers,
of Boston, once put an equal number of black bass
and trout of different sizes in a large aquarium to discover the survival of the fittest, giving no food, but
leaving them to prey on each other; and in spite of
all the sharp spines and protecting scale armor of the
bass, the trout had equal honors! Out of two even
dozen four of each survived.

As long ago as 1748, the Russian naturalist, George
Stellar, made known the salmonidæ of the Pacific
coast. In 1804, Lewis and Clark, American explorers,
added some Rocky Mountain species. In 1855, Dr.
Suckley, of the Pacific Railway Survey, gave a list of
seventeen peculiar to the waters of Washington and
Oregon. " Hallock's Gazetteer " enumerated and described some twenty or more recognized species in
1877; at which date ichthyology was hardly out of
kindergarten. Since then, immense strides have been
made in the pursuit of this science, chiefly under the
tutelage of the inimitable United States Fish Commission, with its manifold equipments; so that it has been

Casting in the Shallows.

able to discover and classify not only the trouts, but all the salt and fresh water genera of the continent.

A recent official summary of American trout, prepared for me by courtesy of William C. Harris, author of "North American Fishes," gives thirty-eight species, besides three introduced from Europe, and not including the sea trout (*s. Canadensis* and *immaculatus*), which was recognized as a distinct species by Smith, Storer, Scott, Hallock, and other early ichthyologists, in contravention of the present standard of differentiation, which is based on anatomical structure entirely:

SUMMARY OF AMERICAN TROUTS.

Salmon Trouts.

Cutthroat or Rocky Mountain Trout—*Salmo Clarkii.*

Yellowstone Trout—*Salmo Clarkii lewisi*—sub-species represented in the tributaries of the Columbia River by *Salmo Clarkii gibsii*—sub-species.

Lake Tahoe Trout—*Salmo Clarkii Henshawi*—sub-species.

Utah Lake Trout—*Salmo Clarkii virginalis*—sub-species.

Rio Grande Trout—*Salmo Clarkii spilurus*—sub-species.

Colorado River Trout—*Salmo Clarkii pleuriticus*—sub-species.

Waha Lake Trout—*Salmo Clarkii bouveri*—sub-species.

Green-back Trout—*Salmo Clarkii stomias*—sub-species.

Yellow-fin Trout — *Salmo Clarkii Macdonaldi* — sub-species.

Silver Trout of Lake Tahoe—*Salmo Clarkii tahoenensis*—sub-species.

Salmon Trout of Lake Sutherland—*Salmo Clarkii declivifrons*—sub-species.

Spotted Trout of Lake Sutherland—*Salmo Clarkii Jordani*—sub-species.

Long-headed Trout of Lake Crescent—*Salmo bathoecetor.*

Steelhead Trout—*Salmo gairdneri.*

Kamloops Trout — *Salmo gairdneri Kamloops* — sub-species.

Blue-back Trout of Lake Crescent—*Salmo gairdneri beardsleei*—sub-species.

Speckled Trout of Lake Crescent—*Salmo gairdneri crescentis*—sub-species.

The Rainbow Trout—*Salmo irideus.*

The Rainbow Trout of West Oregon—*Salmo irideus masoni*—sub-species.

The Rainbow Trout of McCloud River—*Salmo irideus shasta*—sub-species.

The Kern River Trout—*Salmo irideus gilberti*—sub-species.

The Nissull or No-shee Trout—*Salmo irideus stoneri*—sub-species.

The Golden Trout of Mt. Whitney—*Salmo irideus aqua-bonita*—sub-species.

Char Trouts.

The Great Lake Trout—*Cristivomer namaycush*—represented in Lake Superior by *Cristivomer namaycush siscowet*—sub-species.

Eastern Brook or Red-spotted Trout—*Salvelinus fontinalis.*

Dublin Pond Trout—*Salvelinus fontinalis agassizii*—sub-species.

Dolly Varden Trout—*Salvelinus parkei.*

Dolly Varden Trout of Kamchatka—*Salvelinus Kundscha.*

Saibling or European Char—*Salvelinus alpinus.*

Long-finned Char—*Salvelinus Alpinus Alipes*—sub-species.

Greenland Char—*Salvelinus Alpinus Stagnalis*—sub-species.

American Arctic Char—*Salvelinus Alpinus Arcturus*—sub-species.

Sunapee Trout—*Salvelinus Alpinus Aureolus*—sub-species.

Blue-back or Oquassa Trout—*Salvelinus Oquassa.*

The Naresi Trout—*Salvelinus Oquassa Naresi*—sub-species.

The Lac de Marbre Trout—*Salvelinus Oquassa Marstoni*—sub-species.

Introduced Salmon Trouts.

German, brown or Von Behr Trout—*Salmo fario.*
Loch Leven Trout—*Salmo Levenensis.*

Ethics of the Woods.

Has anyone ever thought of the trout as a great moral agent, a conservator of human welfare, as well as a contributor to sport? If not, why not?

Let us consider: Has not this universal favorite among game-fishes posed for decades as an economic factor to increase the revenues of States and replenish depleted exchequers? Has he not led the prospector and explorer up the unmapped defiles to the crown of the divide and discovered rare plants, timber tracts, precious ores, and water-powers? Has he not stimulated a love for nature, made men good, virtuous, and humane? Given occupation to idlers, lured loafers from demoralizing environment, filled libraries with poetry, *belles lettres*, and an angling bibliography as unique as it is entertaining? Has he not, in fact, been a potential instrument to distribute population over the wilderness places, and so filled up the Arcadian recesses of the Catskills, the Adirondacks, the White Mountains, the Appalachians, the Rockies, and the Cascades with cottages, parks, and summer hotels, where the worker and wage-earner may rest from their labors and the butterflies of fashion find a healthful and æsthetic elysium?

Reflecting in its piebald garb the iridescence of the gauze-winged ephemera and parti-colored flowers which bespangle its sequestered haunts in the leafy month of June, it inspires poets, generates good-fellow-

ship, soothes the sullen moods of hermits, and makes
good comrades of us all. It is associated with nature
in her most winsome phases, and none can cultivate
its acquaintance without becoming the better man.
With a good supper at hand in a rustic camp, after a
tiresome day, orisons and benisons rise spontaneously.

Insects as Food.

Oh, leafy June! animate with countless insect forms!
Beneath each maturing leaf bursts the opening chrysa-
lis. Upon the flux of the eddy floats the empty caddis boats, their whilom tenants already translated to
the upper ether. Fleets of gnat-rafts, tossed about and
broken up by the tumbling foam of the cascades re-
lease the myriads of inexorable midgets, which pursue
the angler through the summer months and vex his
waking hours. Gaunt mosquitoes wriggle out of their
swaddling clothes to pipe their resurrection-song and
range afar in quest of blood. Wherever we turn,
whether on land or water, under this decaying leaf or in
that rotten log, in the folds of the alder leaves, trees,
and willows which overhang the streams, among the
succulent weeds which carpet the ponds and river-bot-
toms, within the mosses which cling to the trees, and
in the corrugated bark wherever it grows, we shall
find in this month of June an infinite variety of beetles,
flies, moths, grubs, larvæ, aphides, worms, chrysalides,
etc., which comprise the main food supply of the brook-
trout and his congeners of lake and river. Insects

and trout are the principal tenants of all forested areas where water spaces occur. When forests disappear the trout disappear, because their food supply is cut off.

The same law applies to the salmon. All salmon streams head in the forests, but the incidents of civilization have depleted most of the rivers on the Atlantic coast. The Hudson, the Connecticut, the Merrimac, the Kennebec, the Penobscot, and the Aroostook, all salmon streams erstwhile, and many Nova Scotia rivers also, became barren long before artificial or natural obstructions barred their ascent. This postulate of food supply would seem, then, to settle the much-discussed question whether salmon eat in fresh water while on their way to the spawning beds. Insects are their chief sustenance in the sylvan streams, and they eat there to live. It would be inexplicable, indeed, if salmon alone of all creatures were not required by nature to fortify and strengthen themselves for the supreme work of procreation. It depends, however, upon the length of rivers whether they feed. If the rivers be short, like those of Nova Scotia, Labrador, and Alaska, the run is short, and the necessity of eating minimized; but in large rivers, like those of New Brunswick and the Pacific side, it is different.

Other Trout Food.

There are some localities like the Great Lakes where insect forms are replaced by other kinds of food, because they are prevalent. Flies are therefore disre-

garded, though the instinct of pursuit being dominant, some trout are taken with flies. For the same reason, salmon roe is the preferred bait on the Pacific coast, comprising as it does the principal food of the river trout during the spawning season of the half-dozen kinds of salmon which frequent them. In semi-arid foot-hills of the Rocky Mountain chain, grasshoppers are the choice. In New England wasp-grubs and lob-worms are favorites. In Maine lakes the smelt is a dainty bait. In Pennsylvania " curly jukes," or water-shrimps, are attractive. On the Jordan, in Michigan, a bug contrived of a lump of squirrel meat with trout fins for wings made an effective lure in lumber days a quarter of a century ago. At other times and places cut bait, trout eyes and fins, pennyroyal buds, and bits of red flannel will catch fish. All the same, artificial flies are killing wherever one goes, and will move a trout at one time if not at another; so that it is begging the question to say that in such and such waters they will not rise to the fly. Early morning and evening is the best time to make the test. The best lure at all times is what they seem to be feeding on, or are accustomed to feed upon. This is an axiom. In forest precincts flies are naturally the most attractive in summer.

Why Trout Chase Flies.

The instinct of quest, therefore, prompts the trout to pursue and seize all objects moving in his native element which attract his attention. Nothing comes amiss, large or small, be it chipmunk, mouse, frog, minnow, bug, miller, grub, grasshopper, worm, or fly, without regard to contour or color, though the more familiar forms are the most attractive, especially in the season of the year when they propagate and multiply. Such being the case, it has always puzzled me to know why the water-sprites (*nepidæ*) and whirligigs (*gyrinidæ*), which skip and gyrate all over the eddies at the foot of waterfalls and dams, are so singularly exempt. I have never detected a trout in an attempt to seize one of these long-shanked and steel-clad harlequins, and the insects in question seem to have no fear of the trout. Why is this thus? Are the things poisonous, or indigestible? or are their toenails sharp, like the Irishman's humming-bird?

Bait and Fly.

Some professionals delight to declare that they never fish for trout except with flies, as if that indicated the thoroughbred. Well? I grant that fly-fishing is the kindlier, gentler, and cleaner practice, though I think the advantages of the two methods are about equally balanced, if one is to consider conditions, seasons, and opportunities, and the other incidentals outlined in the books. One will often carry where the other fails. It is not beyond depth to say that if the *soi disant* fly-caster sticks doggedly to his high perch, despising the other, he will some day have to depend on his camp companion to feed the frying-pan. There are lots of fake anglers, especially at the tournaments. There are prize-winners at the score who are dunces on the riverside.

But what is fly-fishing *in esse*? I am always shy of the angler who talks of the advantage of shotting his fly and letting it sink a foot or two. That man is not a fly-fisher in fact. Why? Well, what is a fly? Is it an insect which dives, lives under water, and sinks to the bottom like a corpse over the ship's side at sea? Oh, no! A fly is a creature of the upper air, now touching the surface of the water, anon soaring aloft, here an instant and gone the next, restless as a humming-bird, and seldom still. Why, the shotted fly has not even the attributes of a beetle, or grasshopper, or any other clumsy insect which happens to have wings. It has no buoyancy or life. It cannot rise or even maintain itself on the surface unless the current be swift. It is inanimate and dead. Fly-fishing indeed! Why, man alive! fly-fishing is an art which brooks no compromise. Cross it with other methods, and you have a nonentity, if not a sterile hybrid. In the same category I place all automatic devices and combination baits. Such mechanical "jacks-at-all-trades" simply demoralize the true angler and kill genius. They are inventions of necessity and not of sport. Now, may the reader pardon me! as this paper was not intended to be a dissertation on angling technology, but a general description of the trout family, and his idiosyncrasies. Summarily, the essence of the art called gentle is to know how to find the trout first, and then to present the lure as naturally as possible, without occasioning alarm. The sequence comes with the play on the line; the reward with the heavy basket.

Fisherman's Luck.

Questions repeatedly present themselves to the craft in this wise: Given an abounding trout stream, why does the catch vary so much with equal experts? And why do not all the likely places on a pond or stream pan out alike? Why do we catch a dozen fish in one hole and only one or two, or none, in another equally promising? Why will one angler whip a stream successfully and his partner come home light? Or, of two men in a boat, why will one take ten fish to the other's none? Is it not because the laws of association govern the streams, as well as the forest and field, or even human communities? Accordingly, we find hermits, guerillas, wayfarers, and coteries among trout, as well as communities and schools. Trout have their social sets and their upper ten. There are royal nibs on every stream who appropriate the choicest feeding-places and the securest holes under the bank, dominating the smaller fish and keeping them upstream in the shallow waters. If your angler happens to strike a school or a Newport set, he is O.K. Again, in lakes and ponds it makes every difference in the fisherman's luck whether his end of the boat or raft lies over the ledge, or off it, or over its edge, or whether he drops his line in the clear cold spring-holes where the assembled trout wave their fins contentedly, or casts his lure over the mud bottoms and weedy flats.

With these few hints, I leave the unsophisticated reader to his reflections, and the wiseacres to kindly criticism. It is never well to crowd a stream; for crossed lines never cement good-fellowship.

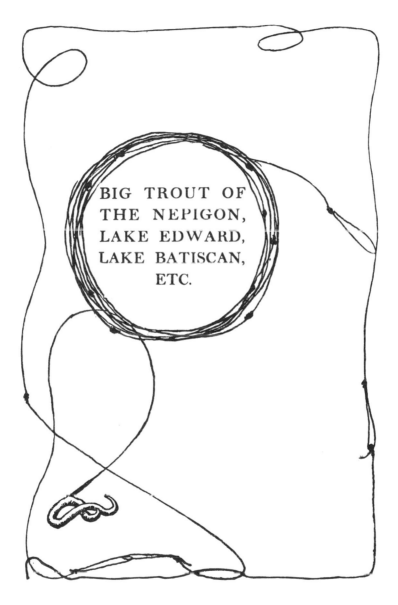

BIG TROUT OF
THE NEPIGON,
LAKE EDWARD,
LAKE BATISCAN,
ETC.

BIG TROUT OF THE NEPIGON, LAKE EDWARD, LAKE BATISCAN, ETC.

CONTEMPLATIVE men who love quietness and virtue and to go a-fishing, attain to such familiarity with the works of Nature, that it would indeed be strange if each succeeding generation of anglers did not make some advance from the previous store of scientific knowledge pertaining to the interesting subjects of fish and fishing. For it is as true in our day as in those in which Walton wrote and fished, that angling is " so like the mathematics that it can never be fully learned; at least not so fully but that there will still be more new experiments left for the trial of other men that succeed us."

Indefatigable industry and rare, ripe scholarship have been devoted to its literature, and though the art is not to be taught by book, yet it teaches many things itself which are not so easily learned in any other school. And since many men of great wisdom, learning, and experience now practise this art, scientific accuracy demands that I should modify the title of this little treatise, at least to the extent of frankly avowing, even at the risk of a solecism, that neither big trout, nor little trout, nor trout of any kind whatever are to be found, either in Lake Edward, Lake Nepigon, or Lake Batiscan; or, for the matter of that, in any of the meres, or lakes, or rivers, of which it is my pleasant recreation to converse with the brethren of the Angle.

The ever-beautiful fish of these waters, whose scientific name is *Salvelinus fontinalis*, has been called a trout, it is true, ever since it became known to the first European settlers of its environment. It came by its vernacular name, says Professor Prince, through the Pilgrim Fathers; who, when they first saw it in New England, mistook it for the same fish which they had known in their own Devonshire streams, and which it resembles in size, form, and other characteristics, although materially differing from it in structure, and especially in the essentially distinguishing trait of the arrangement of teeth upon the vomer. The newcomers were evidently delighted to think that the rivers in the new land, like those of the old, were trout streams, and they gave the fish found in them the name that most nearly reminded them of a form which existed in the mother country, notwithstanding some external differences, such, for instance, as those in the coloration of the spots.

The fact that this charming so-called trout of American waters is not a true *Salmo*, but a char, need not, it has well been said, occasion any sorrow to the angler or to the lover of the attractive fish, since all the members of this group of salmonoids are noted not only for their beauty and grace, but also for their game qualities; and an eminent ichthyologist has declared that "no higher praise can be given to a salmonoid than to call it a char."

Whatever disappointment may be caused the American disciple of the gentle Isaak, by the knowledge that the trout of the "Complete Angler" is a different fish from *fontinalis*, it must not be forgotten that Walton pays quite a compliment to the char, testifying to its "high esteem with persons of great note." The dear old Master Angler was wrong in his supposition that this special *Salvelinus* was only to be found in Lake Windermere, for it is now known to exist in many of the other lakes of the British Isles, and the same variety is said to have been recognized in some of the waters of continental Europe. Though an exceedingly handsome fish, like our own *fontinalis*, Walton's char neither attains to the size of its close congener of the New World, nor yet affords as good sport to the angler; only rarely taking the fly, and being usually caught by trolling with a minnow, on a long line, sunk deep in the water. Our own beautiful char may never succeed in throwing off its domestic appellation of speckled trout, or American brook trout, and since this is so, and that a rose by any other name smells just as sweet, I shall, for convenience sake, make use of such common name, as many others now do, who have no more intention or desire than I have to intimate that this favorite fish is really a trout, or anything more or less than a char, and one of the most elegant, most gamy, and in every way most desirable members of that highly favored species.

Sir Humphry Davy has left us a description of the leading type of the European char, from which we may glean some idea of its brilliant coloring, though British testimony is not wanting to establish the fact that, in the richness of its livery, it still falls short of the glorious apparel of the American brook trout. In fact, no purely British fish, says the author of a paper in *Blackwood's* on "Fontinalis in Scotland," can boast the hues which deck the *fontinalis*. Never, he says, have we seen such gorgeous and brilliant coloring in any finny creature, excepting, perhaps, in some of the quaint tropical varieties from the Caribbean Sea, which are shown to the traveller by negro fishermen in Jamaica.

Sir Humphry Davy had no personal knowledge of our American brook trout, and it is therefore not surprising to read that he had never seen more beautiful fish than the European char, " which, when in perfect season, have the lower fins and the belly of the brightest vermilion, with a white line on the outside of the pectoral, ventral, anal, and lower part of the caudal fin, and with vermilion spots, surrounded by the bright olive shade of the sides and back." Those who have been

privileged to examine the brilliant flaming red bands upon the lower part of the sides of some of Canada's Alpine char, in the spawning season, and especially of the newly named *Salvelinus Oquassa Marstonii*, will see that there is a close resemblance between the appearance of some of the American and European chars, though beautiful as all of these are, no other one of them that has yet been described is arrayed in such shades of olive and purple and crimson and gold, as the large specimens of fontinalis found in the cool, clear waters of Northern Maine and the Dominion of Canada.

Let us carefully examine a newly caught specimen of the Lake Edward trout, fresh from the rapids of the River Jeannotte—the outlet of the big lake—where its monster fish descend in the latter part of August, in search of their spawning-beds. During the heat of the midsummer months we angle in vain for this beautiful creature upon the surface of the water. After the manner of his near kinsman, the char of Windermere and Geneva—*Salvelinus Alpinus*—the gay cavalier seeks the cool depths of the spring-fed lake, whence the most deftly cast flies fail to attract him. Minnows compose his daily menu, and with a cool summer-resort and plenty of good food, he has no inclination to trouble himself with what is disturbing the surface of the water. In the comparatively swift rapids of the picturesque discharge, fontinalis, finding no minnows upon which to feed, is successfully tempted by the fluttering fly to " spring from the deep and try aërial ways." Here the giant specimens of the Lake Edward char, which attain a size rarely to be met in running water, rise freely to the artificial lures which were cast in vain over the bosom of the lake. Here, too, as in the Nepigon and the Montmorenci, at this season of the year, the American brook trout is found in his most gorgeous apparel. His whole being is aflame with burning passion and

28

nuptial desire, which reveal themselves in the fiery flushes of deepest crimson upon his shapely sides and lower fins. The creamy white margins of the pectoral, anal, and ventral fins distinctly mark the course of the fish in the dark water, and form a striking contrast to his olive-colored and vermiculated back and dorsal fin. Here, he has caught the varying tints of the submerged rocks, and of the forest-clad mountains which form the basin of the lake, and in the brilliant brocade of his spotted sides he reflects the gold of the setting sun, and the purple sheen of the distant hills. The partner of his spawning joys and sorrows lacks much of his flaming indication of sexual ambition, but is shapely and jewel-bedecked and beautiful beyond compare. If even Solomon in all his glory was not arrayed like one of these richly colored spawning males, the female fish, with the brilliant silver of its burnished sides, marked with orange and purple spots—their centres often dotted with crimson—is the very embodiment of grace and beauty.

Unlike some of the fickle fair amongst the fishes of Oppian's Halieutics, the big trout of these northern lakes are always found in couples upon the spawning-beds, and so closely attendant are they upon each other's movements, that the spouse of a hooked fish may often be seen swimming around the struggling captive, as though anxious to aid it to be free, and has sometimes been taken in the same landing-net.

During the latter half of August and the whole of September, these large fish rise very freely to ordinary trout flies in the Jeannotte, and have been taken there over seven pounds in weight. Fish from two to five pounds are quite common in all the upper pools of the river at this season, and sometimes the angler may enjoy the sport of playing two or three of them at the same time. They are extremely gamy, and often break water several times before being brought to net. In spring and summer, not one of these large fish is to be found in the stream, though there are plenty of fingerlings ready to seize the angler's flies. The big fellows are all in the big lake. They grow big because of the large extent of spring-fed water in which they roam, and also because of the abundant food supply furnished them by the innumerable shoals of minnows.

The lack of much insect food for fish at Lake Edward is perhaps responsible for the habits of its trout. At all events, the large ones are not to be seduced by insect lures until they withdraw to the shallower water of the spawning-beds in the stream below. In springtime they often come pretty near to the surface of the lake, when they chase the vast shoals of minnows into somewhat shallow water. The frightened little fish fly by thousands in front of their pursuers, and as they spring into the air and fall back into the lake, the splash that they make resembles the sound of a heavy fall of hail. A live minnow is a good bait, and catches of four and five pound fish are of daily occurrence here in the spring of the year. Worms and other ordinary bait are used with good result, and so are mice, frogs,

"*Evening firelight stories.*"

and even pieces of pork. Trolling, either with the spoon, the phantom minnow, or a dead-fish bait, is also very successful. These monster char will readily take a very large size pike-spoon, and will not even refuse to make a meal of the young of their own species.

In all probability there are larger fish in Lake Edward than any that have been taken out of it, and if reliance can be placed upon the stories of the big ones which have been hooked and lost there, the size of its speckled trout is not exceeded in any Canadian stream or lake.

Throughout the northern part of the continent there are a series of favored waters where gigantic specimens of *Salvelinus fontinalis*, at least equalling those caught in Lake Edward, in size and gorgeousness of coloring, and sometimes exceeding them in gameness, are still to be found. These lakes and rivers are situated, for the most part, amid the mountains of the Laurentian chain, which extends from the north of Lake Superior to the sea-coast of Labrador, though some of them occur on the north of the water-shed dividing the waters of Hudson's Bay from those of the Gulf of St. Lawrence. Much confusion has been caused by the application of the name "trout," as well to the namaycush or christivomer as to *Salvelinus fontinalis*, and many reports of large trout in northern waters have been found, upon investigation, to refer to the so-called gray or lake trout, or namaycush. Speckled trout of three to nine pounds in weight are reported, however, to have been taken in nets in Lake

Wahwanichi, a beautiful mere about the size of Lake Edward, namely, twenty miles long by one to three wide.

In the Hamilton River, above the Grand Falls, in the interior of Labrador, there is, according to Mr. Low, the well-known explorer, the finest trout-fishing in Canada —all large fish, none under three pounds, and from this to seven pounds, and plenty of them in all the rapids.

Several of the rivers flowing from the north into Lake Superior also contain very large trout. Professor Ramsay Wright, of the University of Toronto, is authority for the statement that specimens of *Salvelinus fontinalis* have been secured in the Nepigon up to seventeen pounds in weight. Accessibility to an abundant food supply and a deep cold-water habitat contribute very materially to the rapid growth of all the trouts and chars, and the Nepigon River and the lakes by which it is fed contain large quantities of whitefish, while the water is so cold that its average summer temperature is not much above forty degrees. The fish have therefore no reason to keep down in the lowest depths of the river, and they consequently rise freely to the angler's flies. The best fishing is to be had there from the middle of July through the months of August and September. The river is rather more than thirty miles long to the Great Lake Nepigon at its head, and is broken by fifteen *chutes* or falls, at the foot of all of which there is excellent fishing. The average width of the river is two hundred yards, but it has several large lake expansions, and its depth is from twenty to two hundred and fifty feet. Fontinalis has consequently ample scope here for the display of all his fighting qualities. Professor Wright's estimate of the size of the Nepigon fish is probably based upon reports of several years ago, when none but Indians fished the river, and there are many modern authorities for the killing of nine and ten pound brook trout in its waters. The standard flies for the Nepigon are the professor, queen of the water, grizzly king, gray and green drakes, Montreal, silver doctor, coachman, and hackles. Even Nepigon has its off days for the fly-fisher, however, and upon these the phantom minnow usually does good work, though it is a question whether the use of any other lure than flies should not be prohibited upon this magnificent stream, which has already become considerably deteriorated.

The Michipicoten, the Jack Pine, and other streams in this neighborhood are probably but little inferior to the Nepigon, and it is by no means uncommon to take brook trout in all of them up to five pounds in weight.

Not only in the country north of the St. Lawrence are large brook trout to be found. Six and seven pound specimens have been caught in some of the rivers and lakes of the Squatteck country, in the vicinity of Lake Temiscouata, which is not far from the boundary of New Brunswick; while others, nearly as bulky, occur in the preserves of the Megantic Fish and Game Association, on either side of the Maine and Quebec boundary line.

What was supposed to have been a record fish, at the time, was assigned the place of honor in the department of Fish and Fisheries at the Centennial Exhibition in Philadelphia. After it had been some time

dead it turned the scales at ten pounds. Professor Spencer F. Baird and Professor Agassiz are both said to have given it as their opinion that when freshly taken this trout weighed at least eleven and a half pounds. It measured thirty inches in length and eighteen in circumference, and was caught in October,

1867, in one of the Rangeley Lakes, in Maine. Some old anglers, and many younger ones who are acquainted with the literature of the subject, will recall the excitement which broke out in the angling world of America in 1863, when Mr. George Shepard Page, of New York City, returned from a trip to the Rangeleys, bringing with him eight brook trout weighing from eight down to five and a half pounds each. Scores of letters were sent to the papers which had presumed to call these fish brook trout—some of them interrogative, more denunciatory, others theoretical, and some, again, flatly contradictory. The Adirondacks had never yielded a brook trout which weighed more than five pounds, and that, therefore, must be the standard of brook trout the world over. But Mr. Page had foreseen the violent scepticism which was sure to manifest itself, and had sent one of his seven-pounders to Professor Agassiz, who speedily replied that these monster trout were genuine specimens of the so-called speckled or brook trout family, and that they were only found in large numbers in the lakes and streams at the headwaters of the Androscoggin River in Northwestern Maine. The big trout of Lake Edward, of the Nepigon, of Lake Batiscan, Lake Jacques Cartier, and other Canadian waters, were evidently unknown to Professor Agassiz at that time, or he certainly would never have attempted to so limit the occurrence of the monster char. Many of the heavy trout killed in the same waters during the next few years were caught upon trolling lines, though some very large ones rose to the fly, and Mr. Henry O. Stanley, of Dixfield, now and for over thirty years past one of the Fish Commissioners of the State of Maine, has a record of several hundred brook trout taken with the fly, and running from three to nine and a half pounds each.

Lake Batiscan, which is noted for its large trout, is about midway between the city of Quebec and Lake St. John, and only a few miles distant from the line of the railway. Dean Robbins, of Albany, N. Y.; Dr. Robert M. Lawrence, of Lexington, Mass., and a number of friends secured twelve brook trout in Lake Batiscan in 1895, whose aggregate weight was seventy-two pounds. The dean caught, by trolling, an eight and a quarter pound trout, and another of the party one of eight and a half pounds. The latter was twenty-six inches long and seventeen in girth. The Hon. W. B. Kirk, of Syracuse, N. Y., has to his credit a nine-pound trout taken from the same lake. Mr. Alfred Harmsworth, proprietor of the London *Daily Mail*, saw a number of seven and eight pound fish from this lake at the Garrison Club, in Quebec, in 1894, and guessed their average weight at ten pounds, as related at the time by the late Mr. A. N. Cheney, in the columns of *Forest and Stream*. Almost all the waters of the Triton Tract, in which Lake Batiscan is situated, are noted for the large size of the fontinalis which inhabit them. The late Colonel A. L. Light

36

killed fourteen trout in one hour on the tract in 1892, their total weight being forty-five pounds. Mr. Cheney and Mr. W. F. Rathbone, of Albany, took twenty-five speckled trout in the Moise River, on the fly, in September, 1897, which weighed in all 101 pounds. Ten of Mr. Cheney's fish weighed forty-five pounds and ten of Mr. Rathbone's forty-one pounds.

Except in the fall of the year many of the heaviest trout caught in lakes are undoubtedly taken upon the troll. Even those that are killed upon a fly often seize it as it is trolled behind a boat. One of the flies used in angling for these heavy fish is the coarse bunch of hair known as the moose-tail fly. It is usually trolled some distance under the water.

The Lake Batiscan trout are exceptionally handsome fish. They are almost always in good condition. So, too, are those of the Montmorenci River, which are among the most gamy specimens known to Canadian anglers. They feed and fatten largely upon insect food, and hence grow strong and lusty as well as bold and gamy. All fish-culturists know how superior in coloring of flesh, in flavor, and in gameness are those trout and chars which feed upon flies or crustacea.

Mr. Stoddart, in his " Art of Angling as Practised in Scotland," mentions an interesting experiment made with trout, some years ago, in the south of England, in order to ascertain the value of different food. Fish were placed in three separate tanks, one of which was supplied daily with worms, another with live minnows, and the third with those small dark-colored water-flies which are to be found moving about on the surface under banks and sheltered places. The trout fed with worms grew slowly, and had a lean appearance; those nourished on minnows—which it was observed, they darted at with great voracity—became much larger; while such as were fattened upon flies only, attained in a short time prodigious dimensions, weighing twice as much as both the others together, although the quantity of food swallowed by them was in no-wise so great.

Lanman has stated that one principal cause of the great variety in color of the brook trout is the difference of food; such as live upon fresh-water shrimps and other crustacea are the brightest; those which feed upon May-flies and other aquatic insects are the next; and those which feed upon worms are the dullest of all. Trout which feed much upon larvæ (*Phryganidæ*) and their cases are not only red in flesh but they become golden in hue and the red spots increase in number.

Professor Agassiz has said " the most beautiful trout are found in waters which abound in crustacea; direct experiments having shown that the intensity of the red colors of their flesh depends upon the quantity of *Gammaridæ* (fresh-water shrimps) which they have devoured."

Mr. Cheney once wrote that " fishes are probably

creatures of habit as well as man, and if they are supplied only with food which is found at the bottom, they will look to the bottom for it and not look to the surface, where the angler casts his flies; so the food question is one that relates, more than anything else, to the condition of the fish, as their habits may be changed by a change of food that causes them to look up for it rather than down."

This constant looking down for their food in the depths of Lake Edward no doubt accounts for the general refusal of its trout to rise to surface lures.

In the Montmorenci, some twenty to thirty miles above its famous falls; in the Ouiatchouan, the stream which carries the surplus waters of Lake Bouchette into Lake St. John; in La Belle Riviere, and in other northern waters that might be mentioned, fontinalis feeds largely upon insect food, and six and seven pound specimens have not infrequently fallen victims to the fly-fisherman's skill.

Space forbids lengthy reference to the huge trout of the great lake Jacques Cartier, a splendid body of water now hidden in the almost impenetrable depths of the Canadian forest; but those familiar with the works of Mr. John Burroughs will recall the story, in "Locusts and Wild Honey," of the six-pounder taken by him at the very source of the Jacques Cartier River, when there was then a passable road for a buckboard from Quebec to the lake. Since the building of the railway to Lake St. John this pathway has become so deserted that it is in parts quite overgrown with shrubbery, while many of its bridges have entirely disappeared.

A pack-horse may get through to the big lake, and here, in its discharge, and in Lac des Neiges, only a few miles distant from it, are to be found some of the best waters still open to anglers in which the big red trout of Canada may be fished for, and may be caught, too, if good luck wait upon the angler's efforts. The autumn fishing is surer, here, than any other, and September is the best month to go. But the lakes mentioned, as well as all the upper course of the Jacques Cartier River, are comprised in the Government preserve known as the Laurentides National Park, which occupies much of the interior of the country between the Saguenay and the Quebec & Lake St. John Railway. The Government guards this preserve itself and charges $1 per day for the right of fishing its waters, and $1 for the use of canoes and camping equipment. Guides cost $1.50 and $1.25 per day each. Owing to the rapid nature of the Jacques Cartier River in the upper part of its course, and to its extremely wild, precipitous cliffs, it is dangerous and well nigh impossible to ascend it to its source, but good trout-fishing may be had in some of the waters that may be reached by canoes. A drive of thirty miles from Quebec over good country roads brings the angler to a farm-house, where he may obtain lodging and guides, close to the boundary of the park, and a few hours' poling up-

stream brings him to good fishing grounds. The afternoon of the second day should find him at pools where
three and four pound trout have been taken, and if he
prefers a shorter trip he may enjoy good sport in the
Sauteriski, one of the tributaries of the Jacques Cartier, which has yielded five-pound trout in the month
of September. Licenses to fish in the park, which
covers over a million and a half of acres, and all other
information respecting it may be obtained from the
Department of Fish and Game, at the Parliament House
in Quebec. Fair fishing may be had in the rapids of
the Jacques Cartier River in the latter part of May and
the first part of June, and though the largest fish do
not always rise to surface lures in spring-time, trout of
a good size are plentiful, and many anglers prefer to
fight fontinalis in rapid water, even though they may
not secure the biggest fish. Smaller fish may be had
all through the summer in the Jacques Cartier rapids,
but the insect pests of the Canadian forests detract
largely from the sportsman's enjoyment there during
the month of July and the early part of August. The
open season for trout in the province of Quebec com-
mences on May 1st, though it frequently happens
that the ice does not leave the surface of the northern
lakes until several days later. In some seasons the
fish rise as early as the 5th to the 8th of May; in others
there is not much fly-fishing before the 15th of that
month. July is an off month, except for small fish,
or for trolling and bait-fishing; and neither the last ten

days of June nor the first ten or fifteen days of August are as favorable to the sport as earlier and later dates. The open season ends on September 30th.

Many of the best fishing waters already mentioned are entirely controlled by private clubs. The angling in the Jeannotte belongs to the Orleans Fish and Game Club, and that in Lake Batiscan, the river and lake Moise, and numerous other lakes and streams, to the Triton Fish and Game Club. The Stadacona and Laurentide Clubs, of Quebec, own waters containing very large fish, within easy reach of the Quebec & Lake St. John Railway; the magnificent angling in the Ouiatchouan is leased to the Ouiatchouan Fish and Game Club; the Laurentian Club, which contains many New Yorkers in its membership, owns much good water, supplied with heavy trout, in the valley of the St. Maurice, while the fishing of the Nepigon is the property of the Government of Ontario, which charges a license fee of $5 to residents of Canada, and of $10 to non-residents, for the right to two weeks' angling. The fishing in Lake Edward is virtually free to everybody, for it is leased by the proprietor of the hotel there for the accommodation of his guests, and visiting sportsmen have no other place to stay at the lake than either the hotel or some of the camps on the lake shore controlled by its management. Charges for hotel and guides are quite reasonable.

Outside of those of the Laurentides National Park, all unleased waters belonging to the Province of Quebec may be fished by the people of the province, and by any non-resident who pays the license fee of $1 per day, or $10 for the season, which is required of all those non-resident anglers who are not themselves lessees of Government fishing waters, or members of fish and game protection clubs holding one or more such leases.

The angler for the big brook trout of Canadian lakes and rivers may make choice of a great variety of tackle. I have had sea-run specimens of fontinalis no larger than those I should love to kill on a five-ounce rod seize the fly with which I was endeavoring to raise a thirty-pound salmon. How spitefully have I dragged them by main force with my salmon-rod and tackle on the sloping beach out of the water that they were so ruthlessly disturbing! At other times, and under different circumstances, I should have considered that I had drawn a prize out of the pool. On a seven to nine ounce rod these freshly run sea trout give splendid sport. Many anglers kill them with grilse rods, and enjoy the fun, too.

The big trout of inland waters may be killed none too soon for some fishermen with just such tools as those already described. When lighter ones will do the work I have no use for the heavy rods. One of nine ounces, short and stiff, is not too heavy for trolling purposes. For bait I recommend the use of one of seven to nine ounces; rather longer than the trolling rod, and not necessarily quite so stiff. Even for fly-fishing in heavy rapids I have used a nine-ounce lancewood rod, ten feet long. My favorite weapon for this work, however, is a split bamboo made by that prince of good fellows and of amateur rod-makers, Mr.

Graham H. Harris, chairman of the Chicago School Board. It weighs seven ounces, is a beauty, and has four or five pound trout to its credit. A five-ounce rod will do the work equally well, but may take longer about it. Though I have never handled such large fish on a tool of this size, I have killed one of three and a half pounds on a rod that weighed only as many ounces, and that is very much the same thing.

A light reel, holding not less than thirty to thirty-five yards of fine waterproof line, with six to nine feet of good single-gut casting and a few patterns of the stand-ard flies already mentioned, will complete the angler's outfit. Neither the large variety of artificial flies nor yet the fineness of workmanship on the part of the tier, recommended by most angling authorities for use in the small-stream fishing of the Eastern States, is neces-sary to the taking of the untutored, uncivilized fonti-nalis of the heavy waters of Northern Canada. Flies tied upon No. 3 and No. 5 hooks are usually not too large. Often the fish rise to salmon flies. If the water is clear and the weather warm, and the smaller sizes are neces-sary to tempt them, there need be no anxiety on the score of the hook if a heavy fish is struck, providing the quality and the temper of the steel are good. I have seen Mr. George E. Hart, the well-known Water-bury angler, kill a thirty-pound salmon upon a fly that would not be considered large for a fingerling trout.

Every part of the tackle should, however, be thor-oughly tested, for a four, five, six or seven pound trout is a wanton warrior. He is not unlikely to break water, though his leaps as a rule are less frequent than those of a smaller relative. As a matter of fact, there is no rule at all by which to judge of the probable nature or outcome of a fight with fontinalis. His rushes, when he feels the hook, are long and violent;

45

he rapidly changes the scene of the struggle from the bottom of the water to the surface and back again to the bed of the river or lake, neglecting no opportunity of entangling the line about stones, or bushes, or weeds, or fallen trees, and of cutting it upon the rocks. If the fish be too much forced, the hook may readily be torn out of his mouth. If he contrives in the course of his rushes toward the angler to gain the slack of the line, he may shake the hook out of its hold and go free. Not infrequently the fisherman is handicapped by a second and even a third fish seizing one or other of the remaining flies of the cast, and in the see-saw game which follows he is fortunate indeed if he preserves his tackle intact, no matter whether he succeeds or not in saving his whole string of fish.

The huge sea-going specimens of fontinalis which run down out of Canadian rivers into the salt water, to fatten upon the flesh-pots of the briny deep and to burnish their mottled sides till they shine with a silvery polish rivalling that of a freshly run salmon, are worthy of a chapter to themselves. They are caught up to eight and ten pounds each, and when impaled upon the hook of the angler offer just as good sport as that afforded by grilse, played and taken under similar circumstances. Many claims to a distinct variety have been made for some of these sea-run specimens, but Jordan and Evermann have not yet been persuaded of the incorrectness of their present classification. For further details respecting these and other Canadian

salmonoids the reader is referred to the present writer's monograph on "Angling in Canadian Waters," in the sumptuous new work of Dr. F. M. Johnson now in press.

Whether taken out of brackish water in the estuary of some Eastern salmon river, clad in silvery sheen, or from the deep water of some large lake, where the fish is found in its darkest of dark green and olive and crimson apparel, or from the rapid of a clear, cold stream, where its coat of many colors rejoices in the brightest and most brilliantly tinted spots, the angler who feasts his eyes upon the newly caught monster char of Northern waters will readily admit, that, though God might have made a more beautiful object than the American brook trout, yet doubtless God never did, and his heart will be

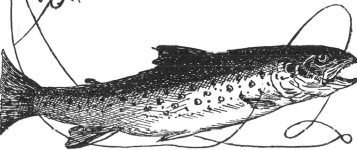

filled with gratitude that such splendid sport is within his reach.

And when the hour comes to fold up his tent and lay away his fishing-rod and flies, he might well wish, like Walton's scholar, for some somniferous potion to force him to sleep away the intermittent time until he enjoys such sport again—which time would pass away with him "as tediously as it does with men in sorrow" —were he not a philosopher and an honest man, who honors philosophy by his virtuous life, and merits the friendship of those who are lovers of virtue, who trust in Providence, who study to be quiet, and who go an-angling.

THE HABITS OF THE TROUT.

THE HABITS OF THE TROUT.

MOST prominent among the trouts—in fact, of any of the American fishes which the anglers of this country prize as a quarry—is the brook or red-spotted trout, *Salvelinus fontinalis.* These technical appellatives are derived from *Salvelinus,* said to be the old name of the char, and *fontinalis,* "living in springs." Unlike many other game fishes, it has but few common or popular names and is known among anglers simply as the "brook, speckled or red-spotted trout."

It is a pure char and the most beautiful of our fresh-water fauna, the more so from the mantle of rose and violet which it wears, the mellow diffusion of which from gills to base of caudal at once suggests the descriptive phrase so often heard among anglers, "the bloom of the trout." Nor is our admiration lessened as we examine his clipper-built form, the bright vermilion dotlets with their dark-blue *areola*, the strength and symmetry of his paired fins, and the broad sweep of his truncate tail, and when we have him hard and fast upon a barbed hook and a springing rod, we cannot fail to appreciate his knightly qualities, his sturdy resistance, and keen intelligence in his efforts to escape from the steel.

Premising that an angler will recognize on sight this brook beauty, aptly and poetically known as "the pride of the rills" wherever he is taken on a light rod and a dancing fly, we will now look into his home life and take note of his habits, habitat, and idiosyncrasies, for he is not without a few odd traits and actions.

Fontinalis—"living in springs"—is without doubt the most amply descriptive, specific name that ichthyologists have ever bestowed upon a fish, for take a trout from its native and highly aerated home and it will die if placed in water of a higher temperature; put him in a large aquarium tank and ice it as you may, and his life is only a question of a few months; the solstice season ends it. At the New York Aquarium, where every appliance for the preservation of fish-life is at hand and intelligently used, the brook trout can seldom be kept from season to season.

Living thus in pure waters, the habits of the trout naturally partake of the character of its environment, if we except the fact that he seems to be somewhat of a gormand. We have frequently taken them on the fly when the head and shoulders of a half-swallowed minnow was sticking from their mouths, which would seem to indicate a tremendous gorging habit; but, on the other hand, even this trait would seem to show their eagerness of pursuit for the most delicate *entree* of their water *menu*, the insects of the pools, hence all anglers with whom to decry their brook beauty is to blaspheme nature, would be disposed to call him a gourmet rather than a glutton.

But be this as it may, when a brook trout is hungry, he is very much like all other creatures of the earth, air, and water, including the human family—he will eat what he can get, his own spawn-child, minnows of all kinds, earthworms and grubs, crawfish and dobsons, all living things of the water-bottoms, and insects of the air that fall upon the surface of the pool. But he is, without doubt, one of the most energetic and persistent foragers for food that our waters contain. We find him dashing over and through the shallows in chase of frightened minnows; breasting the wild waters of the rapids while awaiting the drifting bug or other surface-washed food, and then again we find him leaping for hours into the air, particularly in the gloaming, for the midges, the no-see-ums, or the mosquito fry, born and fledged by the rays of a single

53

day's summer sun. He has been charged with nasti-
ness of appetite because small snakes are eaten by
him. Why not eat them ? The Chinaman loves his
puppy pottage, the Mexican Indian his grasshopper
pudding, and the Southern negro his carrion buzzard
stew. The trout will not eat carrion food of any description, yet the French Creole of Louisiana is said
to hang his wild duck outside the kitchen walls until the atmosphere is soaked with the fowl's decaying
odors, before he cooks and eats it. Again, I very
much doubt if a trout could be tempted to nibble at
a thread of boiled sauer-kraut or even a crumb of a
Welsh-rarebit, at Limburger cheese or a Spanish olla-
podrida. Delicacy of taste and appetite, *per se*, are
seldom, if ever, correlative, but both are strongly, and
often strangely, individualized in all creatures of this
world's habitat.

The habits of the trout being born of the springs,
with an environment, the beauty and almost kaleidoscopic condition of which, changing with every glint of
a sunbeam through the foliage, are, as has been noted,
in touch and quality with its habitat. He seeks the
purest portions of the home stream, loving the white-
capped aeration of the strong currents, and the mouths
of the little rill-like tributaries which not only bring
down food for his well-developed appetite, but a fresh
supply of oxygen for his arterial system. Whenever he is found in a pool of quiet water, a long stretch
of which often exists in large trout-streams, he is less

forceful in action, lazily and leisurely taking the surface lure, and robing himself with a more subdued coloration, which latter, however, seems to illuminate the vermilion spots on its body and deepen the glow of the blue *areola* around each dotlet tinged with a scarlet hue.

Among the fly-fishermen for trout we often hear these characteristic phrases: "He is a slow striker," or "a quick striker," and these qualities when applied to the methods of an angler seem to satisfy his brethren of the craft as to the reasons for success, or the lack of it, in the rodster under discussion. Experience has shown, however, that slow or quick striking on the part of the angler has much less to do with success in scoring than the well-established fact that trout of different waters, even of the same waters where the physical conditions are changing with nearly every rod of its downpour, have varied ways of taking a fly when it is deftly thrown to them. In long, quiet pools overhung with alder growth from which insects are falling constantly the trout has the habit of coming leisurely to the surface, lazily as it were, taking the fly in its mouth in a manner indicating a duty rather than a physical necessity, closing its jaws slowly upon the feathers and then quietly turning tail and returning to its lair below. Now, such fish are a glory to the "slow striker"; he will creel every one of them that rises to his flies. But, then and again, taking the same stream, just above this quiet pool, where a strong rapid is boil-

ing and foaming over the rocks in mid-stream, and
"the slow striker" is all afield. A quick eye with the
nerves all aglow, an instantaneous turn of the wrist
when the slightest swirl in the water is seen, or the
faintest pluck at the feathers is felt, are the only assur-
ances of a successful outing.

Much discussion arose, some years ago, as to the
trout flopping its tail at a floating bug, in its efforts to
disable or drown it and thus render its prey more easy
to capture. In rapid or turbulent waters this never
occurs; in a large quiet one it has been my good fortune to witness it nearly every day for about a fortnight. This delightful experience was awarded me on
the Ontonagon River, some fifteen miles from Waters-
meet, Mich. The trout, averaging about half a pound
each, lived in a pool with but little current, nearly
300 feet in length and fifty in breadth, the banks of
which were densely grown with large alders, the
branches overhanging some six or eight feet on each
side of the pool. The trout seemed to be loitering
expectant under the shadows of the alders for falling
insects, which now and then would drop into the
water. There was no rush, no flash in the pool of a
velvet-robed, red-dotted arrow, but a sluggish coming
to the surface of a sombre fin with a sort of aristocratic
leisure, self-satisfied and confident of success, but a
seeming indifference as to the result. It would open
its relatively ponderous jaws, gulp down the insect, and
leisurely turn tail for the bottom. At least one out of

every five of these trout, as if more lazy or less hungry than its congeners of the pool, would rise nearly to the surface and flop its tail over the floating bug, seldom if ever missing its aim, and so far as I could see, the insect being under water, secured its prey at every sweep of the caudal fin. I noted that the fish with this habit were always, seemingly, the largest trout in the swim, hence their sluggish, lazy way of "taking things as they come," even food or anything else of material value in the economy of fish-life.

Since the days of old Juliana Benners of 1486, who wrote the first printed book on fishing, writers on angling have described the trout as a leaping fish when on the hook, with acrobatic efforts to free themselves from it. No angling outing could be described or a monograph written on this fish without an allusion to his rapid, aerial, and ofttimes successful gyrations to escape. In a trout-angling experience of about half a century but one instance of a trout, when hooked, leaping into the air, on a slack line, has occurred to me. True, this fish, when tightly held, will come to the surface, with its head and part of its body out of the water, and sometimes with the entire body at length on the surface as it fights frantically to escape, but the angler's rod held tightly and upward causes this; given a slack line and the trout will surge deep. On the one occasion when the exception above noted occurred, the trout was struck in the middle of a small pool, and a bowlder protruded its head from the surface on the left side about six inches with a breadth of two feet. Holding tightly, the fish surged deep to the left, and when within a foot of the rock, and unable to go around its lower side because of the strain of the line, and fearing still more its human enemy in front, the fish suddenly leaped into the air on a slack line, and over the top of the bowlder, but this unusual strategic action did not save him; in a few moments he was in my creel.

The size of a trout at its different stages of growth depends upon the area of the water in which it lives, the food therein, and vigor and health of the individual, hence this fish and all other species show characteristic and personal physical traits: some are large and vigorous for their age; others are stunted and feeble, in fact, the natural law of the "survival of the fittest" is supreme among the fauna of the world, whether of the air, the water, or the land, extending, as all know, to the genus *homo*. Hence it is somewhat difficult to decide upon the age of a trout from its size, weight, coloration, or specific form, but, as a rule, the average growth of a trout is about one ounce for the first year, eight to ten ounces in two years, and one pound in three years. These sizes are naturally and relatively increased where their habitat is fully supplied with food and where the water is of higher temperature than in the pure spring streams. For instance, the trout of the Rangeley Lakes in Maine grow to the weight of ten pounds or more; they are pure *Salvelinus fontinalis*,

"Dashing down stream." (*Beaverkill.*)

a classification which some anglers have been disposed to doubt. These trout have become acclimated in the Rangeleys, and, doubtless, their scions from generation to generation and for thousands of years have transmitted to those of the present day the constitutional aptitude to adapt themselves to the higher temperature of these lakes, where food is plenty and constant foraging for it not imperative, as it is in smaller mountain-streams and other waters.

On the approach of the spawning season, which usually occurs in September, October, and November, but is dependent upon the latitude and temperature of the stream or pond, the trout makes its way upward nearly to the sources of the clear, cold spring water brooks, giving preference to those that flow rapidly over gravelly bottoms. Here it selects a spot near the bank and the female flops with the tail the sand from her nest and uses her nose to push the gravel aside, thus forming a slightly concave hollow, in which she deposits her eggs, and the male emits the milt upon them almost at the same time. The parent trouts leave their nests immediately after the act of spawning is completed, giving no parental care to either the ova or their young, a trait so beautifully exhibited by the black-bass, the sunfish, and the lowly "catty." In about an average of eighty days, qualified by the temperature of the water—125 days in that of 37° F., and fifty days in 50° F.—the young are hatched and the fry thenceforth take care of themselves as best they may, the food-bag, or more properly the umbilical sac, which is attached to their bellies, sustaining life for thirty to forty days. It is estimated that not more than five per cent. of the young trout hatched in native waters escape from their enemies and attain maturity; by fish-culture methods, to which we are indebted for the perpetuation of the trout, a percentage of eighty to ninety per cent. is ordinarily reached.

In studying the trout physiologically, we find that its senses are not more acutely developed than those of the other so-called game fishes, in fact, not as much so as those of the small-mouthed black-bass, a fish as quickly alarmed or as " skittish " as the trout, but with more varied and intelligent resources for escape from the hook. There is no question, however, as to the high development of the senses of sight, taste, and hearing in the trout. He is always on the alert for food or ene-mies, with his head up-stream, poising in silence and beauty of form, and, at times, as motionless, seemingly ossified, as a brook-pickerel, which of all fishes is the most statuesque in repose, and one of the swiftest in action. Every angler is aware of the danger of having the shadow of his body, his uplifted rod, or that of his line thrown across a quiet pool; instant alarm and speeding to his home lair, like a thread of fire, is the result. We have seen a trout shy and dart downward at the shadow of a butterfly fluttering over the water, and a low-skimming swallow will send this brook beauty of ours frantically up and down, or crosswise

the pool. No other fish, to my knowledge, is so affected by shadows on the water.

The sense of taste in the trout is more fully attuned
to nicety than that possessed by many other fishes. If
the lure used to entice him be dead, it must be fresh
and sweet; he touches nothing that is not pure and
clean. If the artificial fly is thrown to him in swift
waters, he quickly recognizes the gritty impact of the
steel and spits it out at once, hence the value of
"quick striking" in rapid streams.

The sense of hearing in all species of fish is a matter
of concussion on the surface of the water. Sit motionless in a boat, and you may sing "I Won't Go Home
'Till Morning," or any other gala song, to the extreme
high limit of your voices, and the trout or any other
fish will remain undisturbed, but scratch your toe
upon the bottom of the boat and, presto! the pool is as
dead and barren as a burned prairie. Approach a pool
from over the bank with a careless tread, and when
you reach it the trout are gone, none know where.
Crawl to the pool noiselessly on all-fours and you will
find your trout reposing without fear of danger. The
avoidance of concussion is the great factor on a trout
pool or stream in getting a satisfactory creel; slide,
rather than step, in wading and your success will be
greater.

Trout feed at all hours of the day and night, yet
it would seem that in many waters their hunger ap-
proaches a maximum as the dusk of the day gathers

on the stream, or it may be, and doubtless is, that as the shadows fall their sense of security increases. It is at this hour that insect life is most abundant, particularly the moths and mosquitoes, and trout will often be found jumping for the latter and puzzling the angler, who is at a loss to account for the feeding fish ignoring his feathers. This is easily explained. The trout are busy feeding on tiny "skeets," and nothing but a gray-midge fly tied on No. 18 or 20 hooks will lure them. We have taken trout with such flies up to midnight on both dark and moonlight nights.

The accepted rule that a white miller or other very light-colored flies are the only ones that will attract a trout as the night falls is subject to modification, for this fish is excessively fond of crickets and grasshoppers and lie, perdue, at night along the banks of the stream, where bushes grow thickly close to the water, to feed upon these creatures. Hence when fishing in the evening it would be well for the rodster to vary the dressing of his flies to that of the black hackle or dark Alexandria. We have taken trout of large sizes and in quantities at the foot of a dam where the water was falling and churning into foam by casting a black fly upon the white area.

All of us have seen trout, particularly as the dusk grows, leaping into the air and apparently frolicking, for no lure will entice them. Doubtless, this fish, as black-bass and sometimes yellow-perch certainly do, indulge in such antics from causes unknown to us.

"Taking the first rush"

Perhaps it is from hygienic reasons, or it may be that our brook beauty enjoys a romp now and then just for the "fun of the thing." In nine cases out of ten, however, when these fish are rollicking, as it were, they will be found feeding on minute winged insects that are floating in the air from two to six inches above the surface of the pool, as the newly born mosquito is apt to do, or fontinalis may be pleasing his palate by a feast on the no-see-ums, which the angler can feel to his discomfort but cannot see.

At night we have seldom found trout feeding in the rapids; in the daytime they will be frequently found there, even when the water is shallow and the sun's rays are reflected from every pebble on the bottom of the stream. This practice of feeding in rapid water is exceptional among the so-called game fishes of our inland streams. The black-bass lies occasionally in the eddies at the side of rapids, but seldom, if ever, ventures into the current except, perhaps, for a dash at a victim, and then a quick return to the relatively quiet eddy. The perches and the sunfishes, which include all species of fresh-water basses, are never found in rapids, and the modest chub, ubiquitous as he is, only seeks strong waters to escape the ravenous jaws of the black-bass, impelled to do so by his reasoning instinct that the black-bass does not enter such waters to feed. So we must assign to the trout the quality of muscular activity and vigor of search for food in turbulent waters beyond that possessed by any other fresh-water

fish.   The wannanish, or ouananiche, of the Grande
Déscharge of Lake St. John, Quebec, a kindred congener of the trout, is the most striking example of this
quality.   In this tempestuous water large rocks lie
hither and yon and close together and the boiling current dashes in volume and foam through and over
them at times at least fifty feet at race-horse speed.
In such a habitat the wannanish is at home, and in
keeping with the character of it shows game qualities beyond those of any other member of the salmon
family.

The environment of a mountain trout-stream is ele-
vating to the nature and mood of anyone who reposes
on the banks of the brook or wanders along its shores,
yet we have been told that fishing is a lazy man's
idling, and the saying has become somewhat of an
axiom with those who do not angle or value a knowledge of the natural history of the water fauna of the
country.   Fascinating as this study is, as it is taught
in books, it becomes doubly so when associated with
an angler's life on the stream, where the phases of ani-
mated nature are ceaselessly changing and with every
change unfolding a new delight.   It is not an idle hour
to study the self-containment and posing of a patri-
archal trout, in his knot-rooted home-pool, or the wild
enjoyment of the giddy troutlets, just out of school, as
it were, who seem to be playing a game of shuttles
with their tails as battle-doors among the fluttering and
falling insects of the stream; to watch the frightened

minnows on the shallows, the poise of expectant and hungry yearlings, or the busy spawners on the gravel-beds; to be charmed by the kaleidoscopic color flashes as the sun rays or shadows fall and shift upon and over the rifts and pools; to note the sedate and overhanging alders, under which the lazy veterans of the reaches listlessly rise to the dropping bugs; to repose in a moss-bedded nook of verdure and watch the curling lips of tiny eddies, or the wild rush of mountain-waters; to enjoy the placidity of hill-environed lakes or to hear the innumerable and mysterious utterances from out of the hollows, from the hill-sides, and from the hurling waters and the depths of the forest.

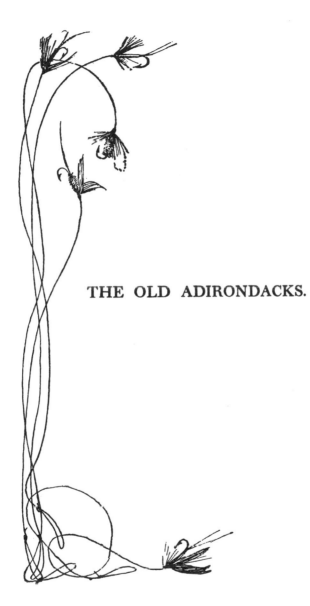

THE OLD ADIRONDACKS.

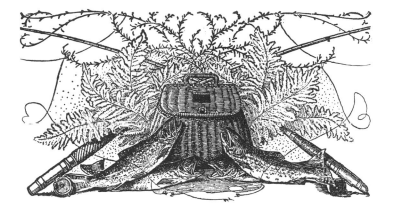

THE OLD ADIRONDACKS.

L AST summer the New York *Times* published an article deprecating the "ruinous publicity" given by Rev. W. H. H. Murray to the sporting attractions of the Adirondacks, and lamenting that this exceptional region should have "fallen from that estate of fish and solitude for which it was originally celebrated." Railroads, stages, telegraphs and hotels, it says, "have followed in the train of the throng who rushed for the wilderness. The desert has blossomed with parasols, and the waste places are filled with picnic-parties, revelling in lemonade and sardines. The piano has banished the deer from the entire region, and seldom is any one of the countless multitude of sportsmen fortunate enough to meet with even the track of a deer." The writer rejoices, and with reason, that Canadian forests are yet undesecrated, and are likely to remain so, "unless some malevolent person writes a book upon the subject, giving to the indiscriminate public the secrets that should be reserved for the true sportsman and the reverent lover of nature."

It is not without a careful consideration of the question in all its aspects that I have ventured to publish my Reference Books. Jealous as I am, in common with all sportsmen, of sportsmen's secrets, and restrained withal by the instincts of self-interest, I should hesitate to reveal them, were it not that concealment is no longer a virtue. The considerations that permit publicity are these:

In the first place, the several great railway routes that have been recently completed or are now in progress—the Intercolonial, the European, and North American, and the various Pacific roads—are opening up to tourists and sportsmen regions hitherto inaccessible. Civilization and its concomitants inevitably follow in their train, and hidden places become open as the day. What would the negative force of silence avail to hinder or prevent?

There is not much danger of the mosquito swamps and inaccessible fastnesses of the Adirondacks being invaded by "good society." The crowd comes only where the way is made easy, and because it is easy. It follows the natural water-courses and avoids the tedious "carries." It halts where the sporting-houses invite, and selects those which provide the most abundant creature comforts.

Murray's book attracted its crowds, not because a legion of uninitiated sportsmen and ambitious Amazons stood waiting for the gates of some new paradise to open, but because it presented the wilderness in new aspects and fascinating colors. It showed how its charms could be made enjoyable even for ladies. It was a simple narrative of personal experience and impressions, written *con amore*, with a vigor and freshness that touched a sympathetic chord in the hearts of its readers. It aroused a latent impulse and provided a new sensation for those who had become surfeited by the weary round of watering-place festivities. And it has accomplished much good by encouraging a taste for field-sports and that health-giving exercise which shall restore the bloom to faded cheeks and vigor to attenuated valetudinarians.

What though the door-posts of Adirondack hostelries be pencilled o'er with names of those who fain would seek renown among the list of mighty Nimrods; what though the wilderness blooms with radiant parasols, and pianos thrum throughout the realm; there yet is ample room for the sportsman, and solitude sufficient for the most sentimental lover of nature. The very contour of the land makes roads impracticable. It is everywhere broken up into mountain ranges, groups, and isolated peaks, interspersed with innumerable basins and water-courses, nearly all connecting. These are the heads and feeders of numerous rivers that flow to every point of the compass, and after tumbling down the lofty water-shed in a series of rapids, fall into the lakes or ocean. These are the sources of the Hudson, the Oswagatchie, Black River, Raquette, Saint Regis, Ausable, and Saranac. It is only where a valuable iron deposit makes it pay to surmount the natural obstacles that some solitary tramway penetrates into the heart of the mountains. The few fertile districts and tillable spots are likely to remain unoccupied forever for lack of highways to a market, unless, perchance, the growth of succeeding centuries drives an overflowing population to the very crags of this American Switzerland.

It has been proposed to make a national park of this grand domain, and dedicate it forever to sports of forest, lake, and field. Why not? Here is a territory of 3,500,000 acres, or 5,000 square miles—larger than the State of Connecticut. Let the disciples of the rod and gun go up and possess the land. Let the girls romp. Let the pianos thrum. Let the wild-wood ring with the merry laughter of healthy women—real flesh-and-blood women who will make wives too good for the sour ascetics who would fain frown them out. Precious indeed in these cloudy times of irksome servitude are the holiday hours we snatch, sparkling with dew and sunshine, from the beatitude of the better day. And what more genial warmth can the sportsman find than the female welcome that greets him from the long piazza when he returns from his exile in the woods!

The borders of the Adirondack Wilderness are accessible at various points by tolerable roads which
branch off from the main thoroughfares of travel. Dr.
Ely's Map, published by Colton, 172 William Street,
New York, gives minutest information as to distances,
interior routes, " carries," hotel and stage accommodation, etc., and no tourist should be without one. I
have found it remarkably accurate in all its details,
though slight corrections are sometimes necessary.
For immediate reference, however, the subjoined di-
rections will prove useful and reliable :

From the southwest the approach is *via* Boonville,
on the Utica & Black River Railroad. A wagon-road
(so-called) leads directly to the Fulton chain of lakes,
in the very heart of what is known as " John Brown's
Tract "; but it is practicable for wheels only for about
fourteen miles, or a little beyond Moose River. Thence
to Arnold's old sporting-house, eight miles, the success
of the journey must depend upon one's ingenuity in
surmounting obstacles. The difficulties of the way
are graphically portrayed by the pen and pencil of T.
B. Thorpe, in the nineteenth volume of *Harper's Maga-
zine*, though the road has been considerably improved
since the article was published. Some few bowlders
have sunk into the mud, and trunks of trees that then
crossed the road have rotted away, so that it is no
longer necessary to go around them. Consequently
the distance is somewhat shortened, and the road made
more level. From Arnold's there is a navigable water-

course all the way to Raquette Lake, a distance of thirty miles, broken by three portages or "carries," whose aggregate length is two and three-quarter miles. Indeed there is a continuous water-course by way of Raquette Lake, as will presently be shown, all the way to the northernmost limit of the Adirondack region. This "John Brown's Tract" is about twenty miles square and contains 210,000 acres. As is well known, it was once the seat of very considerable iron-works which afterward failed in the fulfilment of a promise of lucrative profit, and were abandoned. Arnold's house is a relic of those ancient improvements. It is one of the finest fishing and hunting grounds in the whole section, though here, as elsewhere, the sportsman must turn a little aside from the main thoroughfare if he would find reward commensurate with his endeavors. The adjacent country is hilly, though not strictly mountainous; but there is an isolated peak called "Bald Mountain," which is everywhere the most prominent feature of the landscape. From its summit there is a panorama of magnificent extent. Fourth Lake with its green islands occupies the central position, stretching away for six miles through an unbroken forest whose farthest limit is a blue mountain-range delicately limned upon the horizon. There is a comfortable house near the foot of the mountain where parties proposing to ascend can find an abiding-place.

From the west there are entrances to the Wilderness *via* Lowville and Carthage, stations on the Black

River Railroad, by tolerable wagon-roads which con-
verge at Lake Francis, a distance of eighteen or twenty
miles; thence by road and stream twenty-two miles to
Beach's Lake, and thence nine miles to Raquette Lake.
This route is not much travelled, and the sport will not
pay for the hardships of the journey. Boonville is the
better starting-point.

From Potsdam, on the north, there is a very good
winter road all the way to "Grave's Lodge" on Big
Tupper Lake, whence all parts of the Wilderness are
accessible by boat. The summer route is from Potsdam
to Colton, ten miles by stage; thence by good wagon-
road twelve miles to McEwen's on the Raquette
River; thence six miles to Haw's, with a very short
portage; thence six miles and a half by road to the
"Moosehead still water"; and thence fifteen miles
by water to the foot of Raquette Pond, from which
there is water communication with Big Tupper and all
other points north and south. From McEwen's to
Raquette Pond the river is broken by a succession of
rapids and falls, around which boats must be carried.
Notwithstanding the frequency of the portages, and
the vexatious changes from wagon to stream, this is a
favorite route for sportsmen, for the adjacent country
abounds in fish and game. Visitors to this section do
not, however, generally go through, but camp at eligible
points, or put up at Pelsue's, Haw's, Ferry's, and other
houses below the Piercefield Falls. On the other hand,
visitors from above seldom descend as far as Piercefield.

Entering from the north at Malone on the Ogdens-
burg & Northern Railroad, after a fortnight spent at
Chazy and Chateaugay Lakes, the route is by the east
branch of Saint Regis River to Meacham Pond, famous
for its trout and its beautiful beach, and thence by
stream through Osgood's Pond, with a half-mile carry
to Paul Smith's, on the Lower Saint Regis Lake, the
preferred and best-known starting-point for the interior
Wilderness for all visitors from the East. It is the
easiest and shortest route, and affords fine fishing the
whole distance. There is also an excellent wagon-
road from Malone to Martin's, a favorite hotel on the
Lower Saranac—distance fifty miles.

From the northeast there is a railroad twenty miles
long from Plattsburg to Point of Rocks, Ausable Station, on the Ausable River, whence lines of Concord
stages are run daily over excellent roads to Paul
Smith's and Martin's, diverging at Bloomingdale, the
post-office nearest to either point. The distance by
stage is about forty miles. The same stages also run
from Port Kent, on Lake Champlain, through Keeseville to the railroad terminus at Point of Rocks, a trip
of thirteen miles. By this route a great deal is saved
in distance; but thirteen miles of staging are added,
and nothing is gained in time, as the stages all connect
with the railroad trains. Whether the tourist leaves
the steamer at Port Kent or continues to Plattsburg,
he will have to remain at a hotel over night. The
Wetherill House, and Fouquet's Hotel, at Plattsburg,

V. C. Bartlett's Sportsmen's Home, Saranac Lake, New York, in 1873.

afford the traveller every luxury, and at the Ausable House, Keeseville, there is excellent accommodation. Both places are reached by steamer from Whitehall and Burlington, and also by railroad from Montreal. Tourists often take the Keeseville route in order to visit the celebrated chasm of the Ausable River, a magnificent mountain-gorge of most romantic effects and picturesque scenery. There is also a route to Saranac Lake from this point, which passes through Wilmington Notch and skirts the base of " Whiteface Mountain," and thence continues on through North Elba, where may be seen the tomb of John Brown, of Harper's Ferry renown. There is a road to the top of " Whiteface," whence can be had an illimitable view of the Wilderness. This route altogether affords the most remarkable and varied scenery to be found in the Adirondacks; and a visit will well repay those lovers of nature who have never yet " wet a line " or " drawn a bead on a deer."

By the other route there is a romantic bit of scenery at the Franklin Falls of the Saranac; but its natural charms are disfigured by one of those utilitarian improvements, a saw-mill. Here is the " half-way house," where passengers for Smith's and Martin's dine. Two seasons ago, while indulging in a post-prandial cigar, I took the trouble to count the names on the little hotel register, and found that they numbered 1,500 ! and the season was only half over. These, however, included those going out as well as those going in.

(When a man is headed for the Wilderness, he is said to be "going in.")

There are two other routes from the east, namely, from Westport, and from Crown Point, on Lake Champlain. Both of these take the visitor into the heart of the mountains, the birth-place of winds and the nursery of snow-fed sources. Here old "Boreas Mountain" dwells; here is Boreas Lake, the fountainhead of Boreas River. Here also are Lakes Sanford, Henderson, and Delia, which are often resorted to by pertinacious sportsmen; but as these are most accessible from the south by the old Fort Edward stage-route, or the Adirondack Railroad, which is now extended to North Creek Station, sixty miles from Saratoga, the above-named routes are seldom used.

The Fort Edward road leaves the Saratoga & Whitehall Railway at the station of that name, and extends to Long Lake, a distance of seventy-five miles, touching Lake George at Caldwell, Schroon Lake at Potterville, and passing within easy access of Lakes Delia, Sanford, Henderson, Harris, and Catlin.

From the south access is had to Round Lake and Lakes Pleasant and Piseco—the well-stocked waters of the famed "Piseco Club"—by a good wagon-road which leaves Little Falls or Herkimer on the New York Central Railroad. The distance from Herkimer to the head of Piseco Lake is fifty-two miles.

The foregoing make up a list complete of all the highways into the Adirondack Wilderness, with two exceptions. One is a road to "Joe's Lake" in the lower part of Herkimer County, which leaves the town of Prospect, on the Black River Railroad; and the other a boat-route from Clarksboro, on the Grasse River, to Massawepie Pond at its head. Clarksboro is an iron region at the terminus of a branch of the Watertown & Potsdam Railroad. Massawepie Pond is within striking distance of the Raquette River, near Piercefield Falls, and is visited by old hunters who mean business, and are not afraid to camp out or follow a blind trail through the woods. There are plenty of deer and trout there for those who will hunt them in their season. Massawepie is accessible also by the old Potsdam wagon-road to Tupper's Lake.

The "circumbendibus" route generally taken by ladies and gentlemen who purpose "doing" the Adirondacks thoroughly, is from the foot of the Upper Saranac Lake, three miles over the "Sweeny carry" to the Raquette River; thence through Big Tupper Lake and stream, *via* Round Pond, to Little Tupper Lake; thence through a series of little ponds and connecting streams, with one three-mile carry, to Forked Lake; thence carry a mile and a half to Raquette Lake, the southernmost point of the tour. From Raquette Lake into Long Lake, with three short "carries," thence through Raquette River, Stony Creek, and Stony Creek Pond, with a mile "carry," back to Upper Saranac Lake. From thence visitors for Martin's Ferry carry over at Bartlett's through Round Lake to the

Lower Saranac; for Paul Smith's, they continue through the Upper Saranac to Big Clear Pond, with a forty-rod "carry"; thence carry a mile and a half to the Upper Saint Regis Lake, and thence through Spitfire Pond to head-quarters on the Lower Saint Regis.

There are several routes that diverge from the main route at various points, those most in favor being from Raquette Lake fourteen miles to Blue Mountain Lake, the most beautiful of all the Adirondack waters; from Big Tupper Lake, with a three-mile-carry from Grave's Lodge, to Horseshoe Pond, Hitchins' Pond, and a labyrinth of lakes and ponds of greater or less extent; and from the Upper Saranac through Fish River to Big Square Pond; thence, with a half-mile carry, through a series of small lakes to Big and Little Wolf Ponds, Raquette Pond, and Big Tupper; and thence return by Raquette River to Upper Saranac. The two last-named regions are equal for game and fish to any in the country, and the Hitchins' Pond district is perhaps the best.

Boats from Paul Smith's can traverse 160 miles of lake and stream.

Paul Smith's has been very appropriately styled the "St. James of the Wilderness." It has all the "modern improvements" except gas. A telegraph-wire connects it with the outer world. It has commodious lodgings for nearly 100 guests, and in the height of the season will accommodate many more than it will hold. Sofas and tables are occupied, tents are pitched upon the

Paul Smith's in 1873

lawn in front, and blankets are spread on the floor of the immense guide-house, itself capable of lodging some sixty or more guides. And each guide has his boat. Beautiful crafts they are, weighing from sixty to eighty pounds, and drawing but three inches of water. Most of them carry two persons, some of them three. A guide will sling one of them upon his back and carry it mile after mile as easily as a tortoise carries his shell. When the carries are long, wagons and sleds are in readiness to haul them from landing to landing; but few are the guides that will refuse to back them over for the price of the carriage.

Great is the stir at these caravansaries on the long summer evenings—ribbons fluttering on the piazzas; silks rustling in dress promenade; ladies in short mountain-suits, fresh from an afternoon picnic; embryo sportsmen in velveteen and corduroys of approved cut, descanting learnedly of backwoods experience; excursion - parties returning, laden with trophies of trout and pond-lilies; stages arriving top-heavy with trunks, rifle-cases, and hampers; guides intermingling, proffering services, or arranging trips for the morrow; pistols shooting at random; dogs on the *qui vive*; invalids, bundled in blankets, propped up in chairs; old gents distracted, vainly perusing their papers; fond lovers strolling; dowagers scheming; mosquitoes devouring; the supper-bell ringing, and general commotion confusing mine host. Anon some millionnaire Nimrod or piscator of marked renown drags in from a

weary day with a basket of unusual weight, or perchance a fawn cut down before its time. Fulsome are
the congratulations given, manifold the acknowledg-
ments of his prowess. He receives honors with that
becoming dignity which reticence impresses, and mag-
nificently tips a $20 note to his trusty guide. The
crowd look on in admiration, and vow to emulate the
hero. After supper there is a generous flow of cham-
pagne to a selected few upon the western piazza, and
the exploits of the day are recounted and compared.
The parlors grow noisy with music and dancing;
silence and smoke prevail in the card-room. This is
the daily evening routine.

At early dawn of morning camping parties are astir.
With much careful stowage and trimming of ship, the
impedimenta of the voyage are placed in the boats.
Tents, blankets, cooking-utensils, provision-hampers,
rods, guns, demijohns, satchels, and overcoats are piled
up amidships. A backboard is nicely adjusted in the
stern for the tourist, who takes his seat and hoists his
umbrella. The guide deftly ships his oars, cuts a
fresh piece of tobacco, and awaits orders to start.
Singly, and by twos or threes, the boats get away;
cambric adieus are waved by the few receding friends
on shore, and the household of St. James is left to fin-
ish its slumbers till summoned to breakfast at eight
o'clock. Delicious and vivifying is the pure morning
air, grateful as a mother's lullaby the long sweep of
the oars, enchanting the shifting scenery and ever-

changing outline of shore. In a dreamland of listless and "sweet do-nothing" the hours lapse away. Cigar after cigar melts into smoke. Lunch is leisurely eaten meanwhile. Through the outlet of one lake into the next, winding through many a tortuous stream, gliding past many an islet, with one boat ahead and another astern, and the mechanical oars dripping diamonds of spray that flash in the sun—what can be more deliciously pleasant—what freedom from anxiety and business cares so complete !

"Halloo, guide, what's that? Struck something? Good gracious, you ain't going to stop here in this sedge-grass ! Why, the pesky mosquitoes are thicker than lightning. Whew ! I can't stand this ! They'll eat us alive."

"Got to carry over here, mister. It's only a mile and a half."

A mile and a half to tramp through woods, mud, and mosquitoes.

Ah ! the lake once more ! This is bliss ! What a relief to get on the water again, and away from the mosquitoes ! How clear it is ! What beautiful shores ! Anon into the noble Raquette, with trees overarching, current sluggishly flowing, still waters running deep. Just here the current is swifter. Toss your fly in, where it breaks over that rock. A trout ! Play him well—a large fellow, too ! Well landed— no time to stop long—we'll pick them out as we proceed. The trout always lie among the rocks, in the quick water, at this season. A fortnight later they will be at the mouth of the cold brooks that flow into the main stream. Look! boats coming up—So-and-so's party—been camping down at Long Lake. What luck? Report us, please. Ah! whose house is that? Stetson's. We'll stop when we return. The Saranac at last! What a magnificent sheet of water! What beautiful islands! See those tents! Why, I can count a dozen along the shore. I had no idea so many were camping out. Bartlett's, at last! We tarry here to-night. What a place for trout! Two years ago, just in there, above the dam, where you see that rock in midstream, I hooked a lake trout on the tail-fly of an extraordinary long cast; they say a lake trout won't rise to a fly. *He* did, though, and took it handsomely. I never had better sport in my life. He amused me for half an hour, and when I had him landed, he weighed four pounds and a half. I was proud to kill that fish on my eight-ounce bamboo.

Pleasant is the voyage around the route. Each day's experience differs from the last. New scenery constantly opens to view. Friendly parties and familiar faces are constantly met. And one need not camp out at all if indisposed. The guide will arrange to stop at a hotel each night. And what rousing fun there is in these wayside hostelries when parties meet! What blazing fires, what steaming venison, what pungent odor of fried pork and bacon, what friendly aroma of hot coffee!

Here I would fain indulge my wayward pen, and in fancy go over the ground once more. Perhaps, however, it is better to leave something to the anticipation of those who may seek a new experience

in this enchanting region. For the benefit of such I will say, briefly, that the best fishing is in May. The ice breaks up about April 25th, and the fish are then scattered over the lakes and streams. The monster lake trout, which often weigh sixteen to twenty pounds, can be taken by surface-trolling with a "gong" or "spoon," and sometimes with a fly. The season, however, is cold, and lacks the attractions of leafy June; but there are no flies or mosquitoes to annoy. In June the trout lie in the quick water of the streams where bowlders make an eddy or divide the current. Later they are found at the mouths of cold brooks, preparatory to spawning.

The necessary expenses of the tourist are about $3 per day, whether he stops at a hotel, camps, or takes a guide. The charge for boat and guide is $2.50 per diem; hotel fares from $1.50 to $2.50.

I was most impressed, in my trip through the Adirondacks, with the beauty of the forest in and around Childwold, the solitude of Long Lake and the Fulton chain, the view from Lake Placid and over Mirror Lake, with the peaks of Mount Marcy and its fellows in the south, with the vistas of woods, lakes, and streams along the line of the Webb railroad, and particularly with the superb prospects from the Chateauguay road as it climbs Lyon Mountain, which recalls the scenery of the Blue Ridge. I found much of interest and information in the talk of the guides of the region. The older guides are, as a rule, pessimistic as to the future of the woods, and groan over the change from the old sporting days. They do not care for the tourist business and the hanging round the hotels, even if they make $3 and $4 a day, or double the wages of a decade ago. The younger guides, who knew not the early days, and did not fish and hunt with W. C. Prime, Kit Clark, and their fellows, find the present conditions advantageous, and welcome the increasing bands of tourists. But they spend less and less time in hunting and fishing with their patrons and more in rowing the latter tamely around the lakes, perhaps accompanying them on a day or two's journey through the lakes and over the "carries." In the more remote districts there is still fishing to be had, and the deer are still fairly abundant. I was told, however, of many instances of flagrant violations of the game laws, and it is evident that the woods are not adequately supplied with or patrolled by guardians. Hounding and "jacking" for deer, while forbidden, are still practised, and the remark of a guide on Long Lake, when questioned as to some infraction of the game laws, that "there never was any law on Long Lake," emphasizes the situation.

But while the Adirondacks are changed and are changing, they will remain for many years to come the great natural mountain and lake resort for the larger cities of the eastern seaboard. They are to our generation what the Catskills were to our grandfathers and even to our fathers in youth, and if your true sportsman must now seek the far Canadian woods for big fish and big game, he cannot take with him or away the life-giving air and the exquisite scenery of the Adirondack hills and lakes. He loses, but his loss is the gain of thousands and thousands of less fortunate beings, to whom the woods and hills bring relief from the heat of summer, renewed life and strength, and a keen realization of the old saying that "man made cities, but God made the country."

Lakes George and Champlain, which are always associated with the Adirondacks in the public mind, have undergone comparatively few changes during the past twenty years, and so do not require more than a passing allusion in this sketch. Lake George is still the same beautiful sheet of water, set in a frame of forest-clothed mountains, as when the first French explorer gave to it from its azure depths the name of Saint Sacrament. There are more villas on its shores, more boats upon its waters, a new hotel here and there, or an old one restored, but summer after summer the lake calls to its lovers to return to its beauties in such a way that they must respond. Lake Champlain now has the fine Bluff Point Hotel, just below Plattsburg on its western bank, to add to its attractions, and the tourist, even if he or she is familiar with both lakes, should not fail to again traverse them. Their beauties never fade, and whether one sees Lake Champlain from the slower and comfortable steamboat or the fine rushing trains of the Delaware & Hudson, which traverse its entire western shore, or steams through Lake George, one cannot tire of the infinite variety of water and landscape which both lakes afford.

September is the month of all months to rightly see and appreciate the air and scenery of our Northern lakes and mountains. Now come days filled with sunlight which does not oppress, cooled as it is by the home wind of the northwest, and now succeed nights whose frosty airs give to the woods and lakes a clearness of outline and to the skies a splendor that summer never brings.

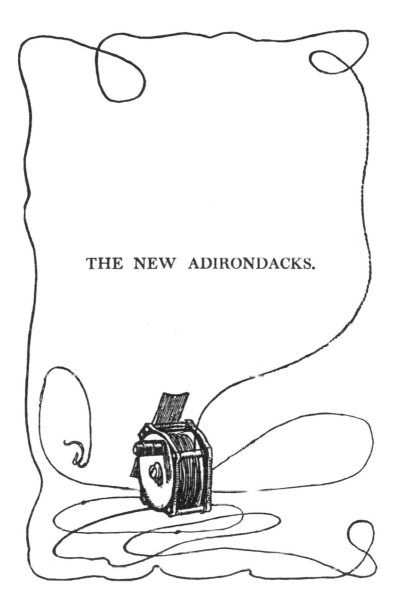

THE NEW ADIRONDACKS.

THE NEW ADIRONDACKS.

THE Adirondack Mountains of northeastern New York affords a striking evidence of the changes which advancing civilization has wrought along our eastern seaboard. There can be seen the development, almost within a decade, of a wilderness into a great summer and autumn resort, dotted with luxurious modern hotels, and traversed by stage-routes and railways.

The sportsman, whether he be hunter or fisherman, familiar with even a portion of the Adirondack Mountains, more poetically termed the North Woods, fifteen or twenty years ago, and who now revisits the scenes of his youth, will find such visit a dream dispelled, for his is the memory of their former wildness and beauty, of trout rising on lakes and streams, of deer roaming the dense woods and drinking from quiet waters, and of a strange, wild life. With this memory, he now finds a large part of the woods region peopled for three months of the year with the votaries of fashion, with steamboats puffing on the lakes and engines shrieking through the forests, with prosperous villages here and there, and the old wild life gone never to return.

I open as I write, an old and well-worn book, dear to all older American sportsmen, written by William C. Prime, and published in 1873, entitled "I Go a-Fishing," and I turn to two chapters respectively entitled "The Saint Regis Waters in Olden Times, 1860," and the "Saint Regis Waters Now, 1872." Would that the venerable author, now I believe a very old man, and long since unable to handle the rod and gun, could revisit the Saint Regis waters and paint us their scenes of to-day. The twelve years which elapsed between his first and second visits seemed to him to have brought many changes, the most marked of which was the expansion of Paul Smith's first little house, built in 1858, and holding not more than eight people, to a large hotel, capable of accommodating 150 guests. On both occasions Mr. Prime had to drive into Paul Smith's from Port Kent, on Lake Champlain, a distance of fifty-five miles. The rare old fisherman and lover of nature, floating in his canoe on the Lower Saint Regis in 1860, wrote as follows: "The day had died most gloriously. The 'sword of the sun' that had lain across the forest was withdrawn and sheathed. There was a stillness on land and water and in the sky that seemed like the presence of an invisible majesty. Eastward the lofty pine-trees rested their green tops in an atmosphere whose massive blue seemed to sustain and support them. Westward the rosy tints along the horizon deepened into crimson around the base of the Saint Regis hills and faded into black toward the north. No sign of life, human or inhuman, was anywhere visible or audible except within the little boat where we two floated; and peace, that peace that reigns where no man is—that peace that never dwells in the abodes of men—here held silent and omnipotent sway. Then came the wind among the pine-trees. The gloom increased and a ripple stole over the water. There was a flapping of one of the lily-pads as the first wave struck them; and then as a breeze passed over us, I threw two flies on the black ripple. There was a swift rush—a sharp dash and plunge in the water. Both were struck at the instant, and then I had work before me that forbade my listening to the voices of the pines. It took five minutes to kill my fish—two splendid specimens. Meanwhile the rip had increased and the breeze came fresh and steady. It was too dark now to see the opposite shore, and the fish rose at every cast. When I had half a dozen of the same sort, and one that lacked only an ounce of being full four pounds, we pulled up the killeck and paddled homeward around the wooded point. The moon rose, and the scene on the lake now became magically beautiful. The mocking laugh of the loon was the only cause of complaint in that evening of splendor. Did you ever hear that laugh?" Again Mr. Prime well says: "One who has in former years lived in the woods forms a stronger attachment for that life than a man ever forms for any other. The affection which we have for the companions of our solitude is very strong. Hence, when I find myself in the woods the old sights and sounds come back with such force that I cannot tear myself away."

I have given Mr. Prime's charming picture of the Saint Regis waters forty and twenty-five years ago so that I might the better, in my feebler way, sketch them to-day, and by this contrast emphasize the difference between our Northern lakes and mountains of the middle and the end of the century. For the change that has transformed the Saint Regis country from a wilderness and the delight of sportsmen to a fashionable summer resort, has also taken place throughout the North Woods, except in a few portions, and will not be long in taking place there. I reached Paul Smith's on a recent September evening by a walk of four and a half miles through a settled country and over a macadamized road from a brick station on the main line of the Adirondack division of the New York Central, which runs from Utica to Montreal. Darkness had fallen before I entered a strip of woods through

which the road runs for a mile before it reaches Paul
Smith's, and cherishing the memory of Mr. Prime's
picture, as I neared the Saint Regis waters I listened
for the laugh of the loon and the wind among the
pines. So listening I suddenly stepped from the darkness of the woods into a blaze of light which flashed
out from the countless windows of an enormous
wooden hotel, and which were reflected far out on the
waters of the lake. There was no laugh of the loon,
but the sound of oars in the rowlocks of numerous
boats, and of men and women's voices " with fashion,
not with feeling, softly freighted." Gone in an instant
was Mr. Prime's picture—vanished the dreams of the
sportsman—and I turned with a sigh to the comforts
of civilization and the atmosphere of New York or
Newport in the season.

I had heard of the "camps" on the Saint Regis
waters, and rising soon after daybreak the next morning, I engaged a guide and was rowed by him in an
Adirondack boat across the Lower Saint Regis through
Spitfire Pond and around the beautiful wooded shores
of the Upper Saint Regis. The morning was very
beautiful. Far to the west the Saint Regis Mountains
lifted their pine-crowned peaks into the hazy blue,
while the sun, just risen, made the dancing ripple of
the lake seem like ridges of burning gold. The wind
blew soft and cool, and there was that vigor and life in
the air which one only finds in the mountains at sun-
rise. A procession of boats laden with supplies for the

97

"camps" plied between them and the hotel, and two naphtha launches puffed hither and thither. I saw the "camps" of Henry L. Hotchkiss, Whitelaw Reid, Charles A. Barney, H. McKay Twombly, Anson Phelps Stokes, P. H. McAlpin, a son-in-law of William Rockefeller, and others. They are, for the most part, really villas, with sea-walls, summer-houses, and every appliance of comfort and luxury. The guide told me that in some of these "camps" there was hot and cold water, and in one electric lights, and it all seemed to me like playing at roughing it, and as if the title "camp" was the only link that connected these modern summer villas with the old free life of the woods. Why does not some modern essayist write of and on "the millionnaire of the wilderness"? One finds strange things in the woods, but the sportsman and true lover of nature can find no stranger bird in the North Woods than the modern millionnaire. I believe that the first of these "campers" on the Upper Saint Regis went in about fifteen years ago, to the astonishment of the guides and natives, armed with a hair-mattress, an air-pillow, and a nameless article of domestic utility. Now he brings electric lights and naphtha launches. It is unnecessary to say that there is little fishing in the Saint Regis waters to-day, and a report that a deer was seen near there this year is not generally accepted. So was my dream dispelled.

But if Paul Smith, with the Saint Regis region, is now solely a fashionable resort, what shall be said of

Saranac Lake, and especially Lake Placid? I had heard much of both places, and I visited both. At the former I found a large village and a hotel—the Ampersand—the most modern, most luxurious, and most pretentious house in the Adirondack Mountains, under whose electric lights and in whose dark wooden halls and rooms one feels as if in town in midwinter, and at the latter I saw a continuous village surrounding its lower end, four or five barn-like wooden hotels, and golf, croquet, and tennis in full force. They have golf-links, by the way, at or near all the Adirondack hotels now. There is, however, a portion of the North Woods where the man or woman who, whether or not in search of fish and game, loves the sense of remoteness and the feeling of the wide woods around can still find sport and an idea at least of primeval wildness. I refer to the southwestern and far western sections, and to that central district which lies west of Port Kent and Port Henry. In the former lie the Fulton chain of lakes, Long Lake and Lake Massawepie, on whose wooded shores, after a six-mile drive through the virgin forest, I found the best kept and most comfortable hotel in the woods, that of Childwold. In the latter region are Blue Mountain Lake and a series of lakes and mountains which are still sportsmen's resorts, and from which the railroad is still far distant.

There are two stand-points from which to view our Northern lakes and mountains to-day. I have treated

them thus far from that of the sportsman and lover
of the woods. The other stand-point from which
to regard them is that of the student of the development of our summer resorts, and of the believer in the
march of modern improvements. There are five men
whom I hold chiefly responsible for the transformation
of the Adirondacks from a sportsman's paradise to a
fashionable summer resort, and these are in order of
precedence: Paul Smith, who entered the woods
from Vermont as a guide in the early fifties; the late
Thomas C. Durant, who projected the Adirondack
Railroad, built from Saratoga to North Creek in the
early seventies; Le Grand Cannon, who projected the
narrow-gauge Chateaugay Railroad, which was first
built from Plattsburg to Dannemora in 1879, and
completed by successive stages to Saranac Lake and
Lake Placid in 1889 and 1890; "Adirondack" Murray, whose ephemeral but flashing pen-pictures of the
"North Woods" first drew public attention to them
and gave him his *nom-de-plume* twenty-five years ago,
and lastly, Dr. Seward Webb, who finally carried
out his long-cherished plan of building a trunk-line
through the heart of the wilderness from Utica to
Montreal in 1891. I should perhaps add to this list
the names of Drs. Loomis, Trudeau, and others who
first directed attention to the Adirondacks as a resort
for consumptives and a natural sanitarium, but I find
that the hotel proprietors and many others interested
are not anxious to have this feature of the mountains

emphasized. With the building of the railroads and the consequent bringing of the mountains within easy access of the cities, and especially New York, the old boarding-houses and small hotels scattered here and there, and which are comparatively few in number, have been enlarged or have given place to fine and expensive structures. Paul Smith's has grown upon and around itself from a little frame house accommodating eight people to an immense building, with spacious piazzas and hallways, which can hold nearly 1,000 guests and is a city in itself. Then comes the Ampersand, a handsome house on Saranac Lake; and then in succession the fine and well-situated Wawbeek Lodge, at the foot of the Upper Saranac; Saranac Inn, at the head of the same lake, and the cluster of large hotels at Lake Placid, beginning with the White Face Inn and including the Ruisseaumont, Lake Placid, Grand View, and Stevens Houses. Scattered here and there throughout the mountains there are also fine or comfortable houses, such as those in the Keene Valley, St. Hubert's Inn and the Chateaugay, Chazy Lake, and Loon Lake Houses on the lakes of those names.

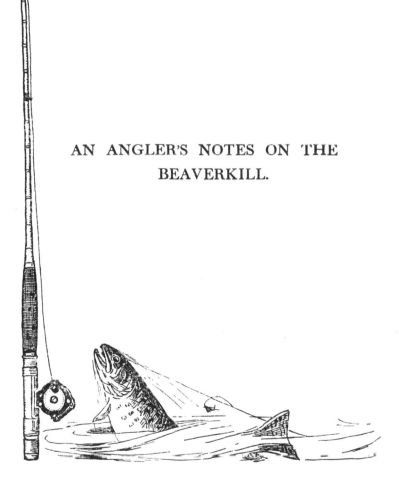

AN ANGLER'S NOTES ON THE
BEAVERKILL.

AN ANGLER'S NOTES ON THE BEAVERKILL.

The Beaverkill.

IF there is one stream more than another that deserves the title of a perfect trout-stream it is the Beaverkill. Rising in the high western Catskills and continuing along the high western plateau, having an elevation of from 1,500 to 2,500 feet, winding and twisting along between high hills and under deep, shady banks and having frequent deep pools, it possesses that first requirement, a cool temperature of the water. Excepting in those rare years when all nature languishes in drought, the stream is broad, deep, and copious. To the fly-caster it is the ideal stream, as he can—after the spring " fresh " is over—wade the entire stream, excepting at two or three very deep pools and at the falls. And the wading, too, is comparatively easy; after one has attempted some of the Adirondack or Maine streams, strewn with great square blocks of granite, the Beaverkill seems a veritable boulevard. The water, naturally, is as clear as crystal. John Burroughs says " there are no streams having the brilliancy of the Catskill streams." The stream, indeed, seems to possess every requirement that a trout-stream should have. The bed of the stream is generally broad, thus facilitating easy fly-casting. The entire stream is a constant succession of rifts and pools, following each other with singular regularity and affording a never-ending source of interest. The head-water of the Beaverkill is Balsam Lake, over on the western slope of Balsam Mountain. I imagine it is a very wild country up that way, as it is entirely out of the way of all travel. One day while hanging around Bill Hardie's, waiting for the buckboard to take me down stream, I fell in with a native from that region. He had some things done up in a bandana handkerchief and was tramping home; he told me it was " purty quiet and lonesome up there, and considerable unhandy for getting things in and out, but he felt that someone had to live up there, so he made up his mind that he would." Weavers is about as far as most anglers go; the stream there is small, but having the same rifts and pools that characterize it lower down. From the falls to where Alder Brook "comes in" the Beaverkill is only a mountain-stream, but from Alder Brook the bed of the stream widens and the mountain-stream becomes a "little river," and from there on down the fly-caster generally has plenty of room for his back-cast. It will matter little to the fly-caster where he starts in, he will surely find beautiful water to whip his flies over.

Changes Caused by Floods.

The great rush of water that flows every few years in the Beaverkill causes many changes in the bed of the stream. One of these big "freshes," as they are called, occurred about the year 1895 and it made great havoc, especially between Shin Creek and Ellsworth's. Just below Shin Creek there was a large pool on Abel Sprague's land that we called the swimming-hole; this was completely filled up with stones and a flat rift above was hollowed out into a deep pool. At Voorhis's great changes took place, the big pool called the "Second Docking," one of the most enchanting places for fly-fishing, was entirely turned about, the pool filled up, and a new channel formed back under the hill-side. "Little Pond Brook," another pool, beloved by all old-timers, was ruined. At the "Big Bend," about midway between Jersey's and Ellsworth's, there was a great upheaval of rocks and stones, piled up fifteen to twenty feet high, and the entire character of the stream was changed. I fear that many a lusty trout met his death in that same "fresh," for I know the fishing was very poor all that spring and summer.

The Izaak Walton of the Beaverkill.

All those old-timers who fished that part of the stream about Shin Creek knew Mr. Theodore Ingalsbe—"Uncle Thee" we called him. It was my good fortune to fish many days with Uncle Thee, and my mind teems with a thousand reminiscences of fishing-trips with him, up and down the stream. Uncle Thee was the acknowledged crack fly-fisherman of the Beaverkill. *He* always caught fish; he used a ten-foot rod, and, as a rule, put out from forty to sixty feet of line. He was by far the longest fly-caster I have known on the Beaverkill, and the dexterity with which he kept that long line from "getting up trees" was a sight worth seeing. I shall have more to say of Uncle Thee later on.

Varieties of Trout in the Beaverkill.

The New York Fish Commissioners have from time to time put a variety of foreign trout in the stream; just why I cannot explain, as the native trout is far superior to all others in every respect. This was well illustrated by a fish commissioner of a neighboring State, who remarked that "one might as well try to paint the rainbow as to improve on our native trout." For a time good sport was had with some "California" trout—as they grew to a large size, they added greatly to the sport—but in a few years they entirely disappeared. I once had an exciting time with one of those big "Californias." One June afternoon Uncle Thee and I strolled down to "Davidson's" Eddy. We were about to start in when Uncle Thee discovered that he had forgotten his landing-net. I insisted upon his taking mine. When I was about half way down the eddy and Uncle Thee was near the lower end I hooked the big fellow. I had on a No. 12 Cahill for a second dropper and the "California" took it with a rush that made my blood tingle. I immediately shouted to Uncle Thee to bring the net. Just opposite a lot of drift trash had caught and toward this the trout made frantic rushes. I was using a nine-foot four-ounce rod. In some way Uncle Thee had entangled the elastic attached to the net in such a manner that we could not undo it, so I told him to net the trout for me. I then began to reel up, the big fellow rushed and tugged, but the little rod was true and the snell was one I had tied myself, so I kept up the pressure and he soon came along. Uncle Thee made a sweep for him but missed him, and away he flew for the drift trash. Again I reeled him up, and that time Uncle Thee slipped the net under him and we carried him on shore; he measured over nineteen inches and was very broad and deep, shaped somewhat like a bass. I have never caught a native as large as that in the Beaverkill, so cannot compare the gamy qualities between the California and the native. I have since caught a brown trout that measured over twenty-two inches that did not begin to " put up the fight " that the California did. For a time a few rainbow trout were caught, but they soon ran out. Then we occasionally saw a trout that for a better name we called " hybrid," a pretty, bright-colored fish with small red spots; they also disappeared. Then, with a rush, came the brown and German trout; I say with a rush because they have multiplied so fast that they now outnumber the native. Comparisons are generally odious, but they are especially so when you compare a brown trout to a native. In appearance the brown is scaly, flat, greenish-yellow, irregular in form, bad eye, homely all over. In the native the scales are invisible; he is gold and silver, round and symmetrical, and as beautiful an object as lavish nature produces. In a sporting way, the brown rushes at a fly and impales himself and then holds back hard and dies limp and wilted. The native, with a gleam and a glint, darts for the fly, and unless the angler's eye and hand are quick, he has taken the fly in his mouth, found it is not food, spit it out, and is off, all in the twinkling of an eye. When hooked he darts about, turns over and over, is here, there, and everywhere. When netted, he is still fighting, and keeps on fighting and kicking and it is the best to-day. It would be difficult to say why this fly has remained so killing when others have had their season and then have proved worthless. Of course, the angler may increase the above list a hundred fold; he may use a Hackle, a Professor, or a Queen of the Water with occasional success, but in my experience the cast that kills is a Cahill for a stretcher and a Marston's Fancy and a Drab Wing Cowdung for droppers. The Marston's Fancy is tied in various patterns, but the one I have found the best is that shown in Mrs. Marbury's " Favorite Flies." But that book must not be a guide to the Cahill, as Fig. 121 in " Favorite Flies " is a very different fly. Fig. 118 is more like a Cahill; possibly it is a typographical error in giving 121 instead of 118. The body of the Cowdung should be a light greenish-yellow, not a cinnamon color. The Yellow May and Green Drake are used in May only, when the May fly is on the water. The Coachman and Black Gnat are used in the evening, especially in June and early July. Uncle Thee always used a Coachman for a stretcher; he was frequently criticised for this, but his reason for doing so, as he confided to me, was simply that he could see it better. A No. 10 fly, fifty or sixty feet away and partly under water, is not a particularly conspicuous object at best, and the white wings of the Coachman were probably more so than the usual drab wing. Orvis's Red Fox is a good fly, so also is the Whirling Dun. The March Brown and Ginger March Brown are to be depended to the bitter end. The brown is more of a cannibal than the native; in fact, most brown trout that I have opened have contained trout, some of which have been a fourth as long as themselves. As food, the flavor of the brown becomes "weedy" after the middle of May and is decidedly unpleasant to the taste, though early in the season he is not so bad. The native is sweet and delicious as long as the stream is up. All talk now about the brown trout is futile; they are there to stay and will remain as long as there are trout in the stream.

Flies.

One of the peculiarities of the native trout is that they will seldom rise, in the daytime, to a fly that has much red in its composition. The most successful flies are the dull, modest-colored ones. The following list is as complete as needed: Cahill, Marston's Fancy, Drab Wing Cowdung, March Brown and Ginger March Brown, Whirling Dun, Black Spinner, Coachman, Black Gnat, Orvis's Red Fox, and Yellow May or Green Drake on No. 12 or 10 hooks. My preference is for a Sproat hook. I like a long, slender point and a fair-sized barb. The O'Shaughnessy is the best hook for big flies, but is too clumsy for anything less than a No. 8. The Cahill fly should have light-brown speckled wings; they are often tied too dark. In my opinion the Cahill is the best fly on the Beaverkill; it was the best when I first fished the stream,

No. 1. Professor   No. 2. Coachman   No. 3. Grizzly King

No. 5. Equinox Gnat

No. 4. Scarlet Ibis   No. 6. Camlet Dun

No. 7. Green Drake   No. 8. Grasshopper   No. 9. Fin-Fly

No. 10. Brown Hen   No. 11. Beaverkill   No. 12. Brown Hackle

No. 13. White Miller   No. 14. Black Gnat   No. 15. Pale Evening Dun

No. 16. Soldier Palmer   No. 17. Abbey   No. 18. Jungle Cock

TROUT FLIES

THE SPECKLED BROOK TROUT

upon, also the Black Spinner. The Orvis's Red Fox is also the correct pattern for the Beaverkill fly, which is tied in a score of different ways.

A brown trout will take anything from a Parma-cheene Belle to a brass button. I met a fisherman last year who was greatly exercised over a brown trout he had caught under the bridge below Joe Cammer's; he thought it looked mighty big and had opened it and found a snake eighteen inches long inside. That was a good story, but not half so good as the famous one told by Jerry Durgin, down in Maine. Jerry was out with a " Sporter " when they " hooked a trout that only measured twelve inches but weighed two and one-half pounds; they cut him open, when out jumped a mink; they caught the mink and took it home and put it in a cage, and by and by it had two little minks." An old friend of mine who lives on the Beaverkill told me with considerable excitement of a fisherman down be-low Rockland who had taken three trout that weighed over three pounds apiece. " Did he get them on a fly ? " I inquired. " Yes," he said, " on a fly, or grass-hopper, or something."

One Sunday in the spring of 1899 I was on the bridge at Craig-e-clare, watching the trout rise to the natural fly on the water. I observed that the smaller ones jumped clear out of the water for the fly, but noticed also that the big fellows never came *quite* to the top, but moved about freely, apparently feeding on the sunken flies. The idea occurred to me to use a small

14 or 12 fly as a stretcher. I tried it the following day and have done so very often since and with excellent result. The sunken fly is much smaller than the fly on the surface of the water.

Casting a Fly.

In casting, I believe in using all the line the width of the stream will permit; the point is to keep as far out of sight as possible. Never cast directly across from you, as the fly will float back toward you and leave a slack line, but by casting a trifle below, the fly floats away from you. Don't neglect the side of the stream you are on, nor the middle of the stream; cast out your flies light and easy, being careful to cover the entire pool, even the very shallow places, for trout, especially in early spring, will run into shallow water to sun themselves. If you have a rise and miss the trout, don't cast back immediately, but wait a minute and then cast with the utmost care over the spot where the trout arose. Don't put your flies too near each other, they should be from two and one-half to three feet apart. Always try to keep the second dropper on the top of the water, there is more sport in hooking one trout on the rise than a dozen under water; in the former you feel that you have fairly earned your fish. If you are a novice in the gentle art, try counting three. One, you pick the flies *quickly* from the water. Two, you allow the line to lengthen out behind. Three, you make the cast; if the cast is a long one

"Softly creeping, lightly dropping."

count two and three for the back cast and four for the
cast. Use your wrist chiefly and don't be afraid of
your rod. Take hold of it as though you could whip
a horse with it, give it life, put force into your cast; so
long as your wrist makes the cast the rod will not be
injured. Remember to take time between the back
cast and the cast; there must be an interval, otherwise
your flies will not lengthen out behind or above.
When you make the cast send the flies out, not down;
cast as though you intended to make the end fly strike
some imaginary object three feet above the water.
The philosophy of the science is simply to make the
rod bend—that's all; if the rod bends to and fro the
line will follow. Try your rod before you run out the
line and see how the snap of your wrist does the work.
Switch it back, pause a moment, then switch it forward. Use your wrist all you can; your arm simply
follows in obedience to the movement of your wrist.
Keep your rod perpendicular whenever possible; in the
back cast the rod should be a trifle to the right, but
the forward cast is from the perpendicular. Put your
thumb up the rod and directly back of it; this will
prevent the sweep from going too far back; in the cast
the thumb is still at an angle, never lengthened out.
The tip of the rod covers about one-half of a semicircle. Look at your watch; let the hours 9 to 3
represent the semicircle; the tip of your rod covers that
part of the semicircle represented by 11 and 2. Be
careful to get all your line and leader out straight and

taut; your flies will then drop lightly on the water; that is the object to be attained, to have your flies light naturally on the water, and at the same time to have your

line and leader taut from the tip of the rod; you are then all ready to strike when you have a rise. Remember, the wrist does it all, makes the cast and strikes the fish. Don't wave your arm as though you were signalling the Empire Express.

Rods.

In fishing from a canoe on still water I prefer a light, whippy rod, but in fishing the Beaverkill, especially when the water is high, a rod can hardly be too stiff. The water carries the flies along rapidly; the trout darts out like a flash; now, if your rod is long and whippy, the tip, when you strike, will dip a long distance toward the water before it sweeps back to hook the fish, and an appreciable amount of time is thus lost; with a stiff rod you save that time and are therefore more likely to hook your fish. *It is hooking a fish on the rise that is the cream of fly-fishing.* My favorite rod for the Beaverkill, especially in the spring, is a six-jointed split bamboo, that measures nine feet and weighs four ounces. That style of rod is frequently used on rapid streams; the short joints add to the stiffness of the rod. A rod of that style, in order to stand the strain, should not only be hand-made but should be made by an expert, and should cost from $30 to $50. Very often a rod that is too whippy can be stiffened by taking a couple of inches from each joint. There is nothing more heart-rending to the fly-caster than to have trout rise to his flies and not be able to hook them.

Landing a Trout.

When you hook a good-sized trout in quick water, never try to reel him up to you, but keep a taut line and gradually work down below him, reeling in as you move along; then lead him back of some rock or in some part of the stream where the water seems less swift; then reel up all the line excepting about six or eight feet; this you take up inch by inch in your fingers until you judge the length of line and leader is such that you can reach your net under him; then take the rod in your left hand and hold the line between your fingers and thumb—you will thus be ready to give him line in case he makes a rush; then lead him toward you from the side, not from above or below, or *move over to him*, raise the tip of your rod until the trout is near enough, and then slip the net under him. Kill him at once by striking him a sharp blow between the eyes—never let a trout die in your creel; then, finally, take the hook from his mouth, and if you have induced him to take your fly on the surface you can feel that you have done a good stroke and fairly earned your trout. If the trout is a big fellow you may be obliged to lead him down to the pool below, but it's always a bit more sport to land your trout in a rift, if you can.

Leaders.

The leader is the most important part of the fly-caster's outfit; the length must be guided by the length of the rod; it should reach, after the end fly is attached, from the reel to within three inches of the tip; the color should be a light blue, commonly called mist color; the strength should be equal to the strength of the largest trout you expect to catch; this you must decide by putting your leader to a severe test; after first soaking it well, hook one end over some convenient object, and then *pull*—don't be afraid of it, pull hard; if it breaks you can easily tie it again. Don't continue to use a leader too long; it is wise to give it a good test two or three times a day. In attaching the droppers, I prefer, for stream-fishing, to put the fly directly on the leader and not on a loop. The object to be obtained is to keep the fly from whipping around the leader. My experience has taught me that the fly stands out better when fastened directly to the leader; this is done simply by looping up an inch or so of the leader just above a knot and then slipping the loop of the fly over the leader, then putting the fly through the loop and pulling it taut; the snell of the fly must, of course, be previously well soaked. In putting on the fly be sure to have the point *toward* you, otherwise it will float on its back. This is an important matter that you cannot be too careful about; watch constantly to see that your flies float naturally and not upside down. I do not like drawn gut, it is too brittle; it seems to dry very quickly, and when dry breaks with a snap.

Sawdust.

There are two subjects that sadly need the attention of the Fish Commissioners on the Beaverkill—the question of sawdust and " posting." The saw-mill at Voorhis's has ruined all that part of the stream from Voorhis's to Ellsworth's for fly-casting; the bait fisherman may be able to catch fish by sinking his worm, but the fly-caster cannot catch trout when his flies float on sawdust or a piece of scantling. Unfortunately for the fisherman, the saw-mill people and the commissioners had a legal set-to, in which the commissioners did not secure their point; this was virtually a victory for the saw-mill. Prior to that lawsuit the sawdust was carted over on the bank, but afterward it was dumped into the stream, and especially so when a luckless fly-caster happened that way. It is sad to think of the beautiful pools that are now ruined—all that lovely stretch of water above and below " Pappy " Dumond's and along by and below Mr. Jersey's place. A movement was once started to induce the saw-mill people to put in a " blower," but it fell through. Something should be done.

Posting.

This is a vexed question. Some fishermen pay the twenty-five or fifty cents; others refuse, and go right along and " talk back " at the farmers. Some farmers refuse all overtures to " fish over them," and threaten to shoot, etc. All this is very unfortunate. It would be a good thing for the fishermen if all the farmers from Flint's docking to Voorhis's would form an association and charge a fee to fish over the entire stretch, so much per day or week, and in return for this the farmer should build small ponds to keep the fry furnished by the State for a year or so, and then run them into the stream.

A Limit.

If that old Frank Forrester law, in force once upon a time on Long Island, could have been made general and enforced, what a blessing it would be to the angler of to-day! What slaughter there has been! Two men killed 700 trout in one day, one man killed 250, another 200, and so on. One Decoration Day, at Sprague's, enough trout to fill a wash-boiler were brought in. It was then that Uncle Thee proposed that we all agree to kill only eighteen trout a day hereafter. The season is too long; April 16th to August 31st is unreasonable. July 15th should end it. How nice it would be if one stream in New York was set aside for fly-casting only, the same as is frequently done in Maine. To think of the Beaverkill freed from sawdust and reserved for fly-casting only. How ecstatic! It is almost too enjoyable a day-dream to permit yourself to indulge in.

The Month of May.

May is the fly-casters' month; the stream then is generally at a good height for wading; the flies are on the water and the trout are on the rise; the birds are flying north and all the air is filled with the melody of their song; the mountain-sides are painted in their exquisite tints, not the gorgeous reds and yellows of autumn, but the pale tints of early spring: the mauves, the steel-grays, the lemon-yellows and pink and soft purple and blue—all those light impressions—with only here and there a bit of red maple or green hemlock to heighten the color. Then to start in at some part of the stream that you have decided upon the previous evening; to feel the rush of water about you and the constantly moving pictures of nature; to breathe in deep the pure, cool mountain-air; the excitement of casting your flies and the constant expectation of a lusty trout—here is a life worth living. How the hours fly by! You look at your watch; it is two o'clock; you say to yourself, "What have you done?" "Where have you been? It seems but a moment ago that you started in; how the time does fly!" What a joy it is to be entirely alone with nature—to feel that you are a part of all that is going on; that the birds are singing for you, the flowers are blooming for you; the lovely violets on the edge of the water, the great splashes of white blossoms on the "shin-hopple," the rich red of the wake-robin and the white and red flowers

A cool spot in leafy June.

of the trillium—all for you! And then, again, to reach the pool that is your especial delight, the pool that you dreamed of all winter. You wade in carefully and take your stand from where you can cast your flies over all the favorite spots, every one of which brings back a memory of some former visit when you had landed a beauty. Ah, that's the life! to feel that you are a part of Nature, and that your love for her is the one great, absorbing theme of your existence. Love and caress Nature, and she will repay you a thousandfold. She will always prove your true, steadfast friend, always trying to be a pleasure and a comfort to you, growing dearer to you and more lovable to you as the years roll by.

Cutting Sticks.

On Sundays, Uncle Thee and I were accustomed to stroll along the border of the stream and ramble through the wooded sides in search of walking-sticks. Did you ever hunt for a good stick, one that was straight and strong and having a good handle? Such a stick is hard to find, hence the fascination of hunting for one. It's curious how few sticks are straight to begin with, and if you find a straight one, the handle is imperfect, and so you go poking about in the woods with a never-ending delight over the pursuit. Incidentally, on these trips, we also kept our eyes open for some big trout that might rise and disclose his "home," possibly behind some big rock or under some bank or other hiding-place from where he could dart out for a passing fly. When we reached Davidson's Eddy we were sure to see some evidences of big trout. Davidson's Eddy is probably the most celebrated pool on the Beaverkill. The stream along there runs in a southerly direction, and just at the eddy there is a high hill on the western side that shades the pool most of the afternoon. It is shallow along the eastern bank, and deep under the wooded banks on the western side, the very conditions that a fly-caster especially loves. It is thus a particularly interesting pool for afternoon and evening fishing. At Davidson's Eddy we would sit down and watch for the trout to rise. Uncle Thee was more or less given to sentimentalizing on these Sunday rambles. One of his favorite hobbies was that time-worn subject, "things always adjust themselves," and many were the stories he would tell to illustrate this, some of them highly interesting and not a few quite dramatic. Uncle Thee insisted that if you transgressed against the laws of God and Nature you suffered, and if you lived up to them you were repaid. "That every man carried about in his own heart a heaven or a hell, the one always ready to please and exalt him if he did right and the other to depress and torment him if he did wrong." Uncle Thee's religion was a very simple one; he had turned against all creeds, he said. "As I grow older my faith and belief in an Almighty Being grows stronger. I find that all the religion I need is the implicit belief that *my love* for God grows deeper and stronger, and that my faith and love shall remain steadfast to the end." The expression of his face showed that his words were true, always kindly and loving, quiet and sincere, faithful and true, and with all a childlike simplicity that won all hearts. Even Bill Hardie allowed him to fish " over him."

> "*He kept his soul unspotted*
> *As he went upon his way.*"

. . . . .

> "*He had time to see the beauty*
> *That the Lord spread all around;*
> *He had time to hear the music*
> *In the shells the children found.*"

A Hobby.

The idea of a hobby is at least interesting to all men, to have some diversion to fill your leisure hours and to look forward to, to dream over on dismal winter days, and to divert your mind when cares annoy. What hobby can be more interesting, more captivating, more satisfying than the hobby of fly-casting? There are a hundred and one features to it—you can tie your own flies, make your own rods, mend, fix, adjust, always some delightful things to " tinker " over or with, arranging your flies and all that, and then the " art " itself. Nothing can be more enjoyable than to wade a stream, to feel the rush of water about you, the constant excitement, the forgetting of all other affairs, the out-door life, the health and appetite, the meeting with other anglers and the telling over of the day's sport. Here is a fascination that will last you all your life, and be a delight to you in extreme old age. Let me warn you, my reader, if you are not a lover of Nature and out-door life you are missing one of the greatest blessings this world affords.

WINGED ENEMIES OF BROOK TROUT.

WINGED ENEMIES OF BROOK TROUT.

SOME idea of the serious loss of fish and fish-eggs caused by myriads of enemies in and about the waters is conveyed in a paragraph of Dr. Day's book upon the British and Irish *Salmonidæ.* He says: "So enormous is the loss which occurs among the eggs and young, that in such a river as the Severn the annual produce of salmon and grilse at the present time (1887) consists of about 20,000 fish. Were all the ova of one female salmon of about twenty pounds' weight to be hatched and attain maturity, they would suffice for keeping up the stock to its present condition." The Severn is 200 miles long and receives five principal tributaries.

Chief among the destroyers of fish are certain birds and winged insects. The common crow, the crow blackbird, hawks, bluejay, some owls, grebes, gulls, and terns, have the reputation of poaching to some extent, but their depredations are much less in our State than the ravages of such birds, for example, as the herons, kingfisher, certain ducks, loons, and fish-hawk. Chief among these is the

Night-heron.

In the report of the Pennsylvania Fish Commission for 1897 Dr. B. H. Warren publishes some interesting notes on the destructive work of the black-crown *night-heron*. In a small pool at Westchester, Pa., twenty-five goldfish were placed. Two night-herons caught all but one of them before the following morning. A night-heron killed near a branch of White Clay Creek, in Pennsylvania, had the tail of a common sucker of about twelve inches long projecting four inches beyond its bill. The head and shoulders, except the bony portion, were eaten away by the gastric juice of the stomach. Dr. Warren examined the stomachs of about twenty of these herons which were shot in June near their breeding-ground, and found fish remains in all of them.

In July, 1883, Dr. Rudolph Hessel shot a night-heron containing the heads of seventy-eight young carp. This bird is sometimes called *blue heron*, and is also quite generally called a *crane*, but this is erroneous.

It is found in large numbers, and in the breeding season forms rookeries which are a serious menace to the fishing waters of the neighborhood. It is extremely shy and cautious, fishing chiefly at night or early in the morning. It stands perfectly motionless in the water until a fish comes within reach, when it strikes with its long, sharp, heavy bill, which deals death to any of the fish kind.

They have been caught in steel traps set in ponds within twenty feet of a hatchery building. The traps are set in shallow water, taking precaution to secure them so as to prevent the bird flying away with them. When a heron is captured in a trap, he should be killed at once with a long club or a load of shot. Great care should be taken to keep out of the reach of his murderous bill. Once I had the misfortune to be struck by a wounded heron, and I am sure that if his bill had struck me squarely on the hand, it would have gone entirely through. As it was, the blow was a glancing one, striking me on the knuckle, but it stripped off the flesh to the very bone. I have sometimes heard a great flopping and disturbance in the waters of our Caledonia trout-brook at night, and upon going to the place in the morning found heron tracks in the mud, and sometimes a trout from one-half pound to two pounds in weight, and occasionally larger, with a hole in its back or side, into which you could put your finger. I always supposed the fish escaped on account of its being too strong and lively for the heron, although mortally wounded. I have seen as many as a dozen six-inch trout in the throat and stomach cf a heron killed in the early morning hours.

In Germany, and elsewhere in Europe, herons work great injury to the fish-culturists. In the government fisheries the regulations prescribe that they must be killed and their roosts destroyed, but in spite of these measures their numbers are seriously large in many places, and owners of ponds trap them with steel traps baited with fish.

The small *green heron* and the *bittern* are also in the list of fish-destroyers, but they are less destructive than the night-heron on account of their smaller size, but their presence about fish preserves is not at all beneficial and they should be killed.

Kingfisher.

The kingfisher is one of the most active, impudent, and persistent of the enemies of fish wherever found, and it is only too abundant for the good of angling. According to Dr. Brehm, the common European kingfisher on the average destroys daily ten or twelve fish, each about as long as a man's finger. In fourteen years a German fish-culturist caught upwards of 700 kingfishers near his trout-ponds. The bird is equally abundant and quite as destructive in New York, and may be regarded as one of the pests afflicting the fish-culturists.

I have known of upward of 180 kingfishers being

destroyed on one-half mile of Caledonia Spring Creek in one season; they were shot and trapped.

In 1884 I rented an old mill-pond in Genesee County, N. Y., posted it with a view of making a trout-preserve, as the pond was fed by cold spring brooks and contained nothing but trout. I visited the pond on an average once in two weeks, with a few friends, for a day's sport. Noticing that the kingfishers were quite numerous, I suggested to the farmer's son, residing near by, and who also watched the ponds for me, that if he would trap and shoot the kingfishers I would give him ten cents each. This was followed up until I found it most too expensive, as the young man produced the heads or bodies of from ten to thirty kingfishers every time I visited the place.

The clattering notes of this bird are heard from early in the spring until cold weather, and even before the spring season is open, as if impatient for it to come. He is never satisfied, being on the lookout from daylight until dark, and is ever ready for a plunge in the water at sight of his prey. He can take as many fish as the average sportsman.

In the article of Dr. Warren above referred to are some accounts of the destruction wrought by the belted kingfishers. Mr. C. K. Sober, of Lewisburg, Pa., found thirteen small brook-trout in one of these birds which was shot on Baker Run. An acquaintance of Dr. Warren some years ago had a large number of goldfish in a pond. Two pairs of kingfishers built their nests in a sand-bank near the pond. In one summer these birds destroyed nearly all the small-sized fish in the place. Out of thirty-eight of these birds taken about streams and mill-ponds, thirty-six contained nothing but fish remains.

Kingfishers can be successfully captured in traps fastened at the top of stakes driven in the bank about trout-ponds or along trout-streams. The stake or pole should be from ten to fifteen feet long. If the top of the stake is not sufficiently large to support the steel trap, nail a small block of wood on the end of the pole. The trap is set, but not baited. When the trap is set, the little plate that springs the trap when disturbed is the highest point of the trap. The trap must be securely fastened to the stake by a cord, small wire, or chain. The birds on visiting the ponds or streams will invariably fly to one of these stakes, light on the highest point and be captured. I have found a small, round steel trap (one without the shank or tail-piece) to be best for this work. One of these traps captured twenty-five kingfishers at a trout-preserve in Cattaraugus County. Of course, the pole and trap should be set up near a fishing-ground, where the bird may think it is a splendid spot for observation.

Ducks.

Domestic ducks as well as geese are great destroyers of fish, and should never be allowed on trout-waters. I have seen a tame duck capture and devour a trout seven inches long. They also feed on the natural food of the fish. Wild ducks of some species are equally troublesome, and especially the mergansers, saw-bills, sheldrakes or fish-ducks.

The merganser is very destructive at all times, but particularly in winter, when most of the streams and lakes are frozen over. They often congregate on small streams or ponds that do not freeze on account of their uniform temperature. These waters are invariably trout-waters. During severe winters this fish-duck sometimes remains on Caledonia Creek for a month at a time. At such times it is very shy, and it is almost impossible to get a shot at them or keep them away from the stream. Trout spawning-beds are also tempting spots for the fish-duck to congregate and feed. I have sometimes found red-flannel flags, placed on poles stuck in the bank along the stream, useful for scaring the ducks away.

Loons.

Dr. Warren examined the stomachs of sixteen loons, three of which were the red-throated species, and found remains of fish in thirteen. Fall-fish, suckers, carp, catfish, and also a brook-trout seven inches long were found in the stomachs of loons killed in Pennsylvania.

On the inland lakes of New York these birds subsist chiefly upon fish and destroy a great many. In the counties of Chester, Delaware, Clinton, and Lehigh, Pa., the stomach contents of seven loons captured during the winter months consisted entirely of fish-bones and scales.

Loons are sometimes caught alive in pound-nets set by the fishermen of the great lakes and on the sea-coast. They are very dangerous to handle, on account of the strength and sharpness of their bill and their savage disposition.

Grebes.

The grebe, known also as hell-divers and water-witches, feed upon fish, frogs, aquatic insects, especially beetles, and water-plants. They nest in streams, lakes, and ponds, usually building among reeds or rushes, and lay from six to eight eggs of uniform color. They are distributed all over the world, and are everywhere known as expert divers and swimmers and generally destructive to fish.

The horned or crested grebe lives principally upon small fish. These birds are so exceedingly cautious and swift in their movements that it is quite difficult to shoot them, but by persistent watching it can be accomplished, as many duck-shooters know. One of the best ways to reduce their number is by taking their eggs from the rudely constructed nests in the reeds and thickets close to the surface of the water. The eggs of the horned grebe are greenish.

Fish-hawk.

The depredations of the fish-hawk are more frequent along the sea-coast than on inland waters, but the birds are often found along our large rivers and over large lakes and ponds. They are usually solitary in spring and fall, but sometimes hunt in pairs, and will remain about mill-dams and fish-ponds a few days at a time if not driven away.

I have known of their taking trout of one-half pound weight from my private trout-ponds.

Dr. Warren examined the stomachs of twenty-three and found nothing in them but fish remains. Fish-hawks are quite common throughout the Adirondack region. Goldfish-ponds are particularly liable to attack from fish-hawks, owing to the bright color of their occupants.

Bald Eagle.

The national bird usually plays the rôle of a fish-thief, his victim being the fish-hawk, but occasionally has been seen fishing in shallow parts of small creeks on his own account.

Audubon states that he saw a bald eagle capture a number of red fins in Perkiomen Creek, Pa., by wading briskly through the water and striking at them with his bill. On the Island of Kadiak, Alaska, according to Dr. Bean, this eagle is actively engaged in fishing, and is most abundant around the salmon-lakes and shallow bays.

Many of the observing guides of the Adirondacks will tell you how they have seen a bald eagle attack a fish-hawk in the air, and make him drop the fish he had just captured from the lake below, and before the fish could strike the water the eagle would swoop down and catch it in his claws; but the eagle is so very scarce in New York that it hardly seems right to recommend their destruction, even if the law would permit it, which it does not.

Barred Owl.

Although this bird is commonly credited with the destruction of fish-food, such as snails, caddis larvæ, and crayfish, it has sometimes been accused of catching fish. An instance of the capture of a large brook trout at the State Hatchery at Allentown, Pa., by a *barred owl* was reported several years ago, and Dr. Warren was informed by residents of Florida, in 1885, that the bird frequently caught fish in that State, securing them by dexterous movement of the foot while sitting close to the water's edge.

The common hoot-owl, or screech-owl, quite often causes trouble. I have caught them in traps set for musk-rats four inches under water. They were after the fish-food of the stream, such as caddis larvæ, crayfish, shrimp, etc. I have seen two or three quarts of the caddis-larvæ cases in a pile that had been collected from the water by a screech-owl, the larvæ being pulled from the case and devoured by the owl.

Injurious Insects.

The damage to fish-eggs and young fish caused by insects and the larvæ which pass a portion of their existence in water, is less noticeable than the injury done by the birds, but it is much greater than one would suppose without investigation.

The larvæ of the dragon-flies, and the great water-beetles and water-bugs are well-known enemies of fish.

Several kinds of water-beetles, particularly the rapacious *dytiscus*, devour fry in enormous numbers, and the great water-bug, called *belostoma* by entomologists, is also injurious in trout-waters. Both the beetles and their larvæ completely devour eggs and little fish measuring several inches in length, while they often eat holes into larger fish. This large water-beetle often leaves the water, perhaps for a little exercise. Whether they fly during daylight I cannot say, but I have seen and secured them near an electric light located within a short distance of a stream.

We do not see and therefore do not know the full extent of the depredations continually going on around us, but when we stop to realize the fruits of our labor and patient expectation, we are astonished by the scarcity of fish and often inclined to place the blame where it does not belong. Nature's checks upon over-production are sometimes more effective than man's most ingenious devices for the legitimate capture or legal destruction of fish, but at the present state of the fishing waters in New York, it is safe to say that we could get along without Nature's checks.

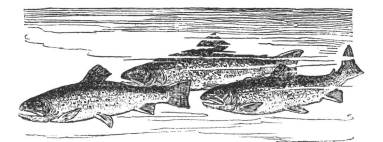

TROUT PROPAGATION.

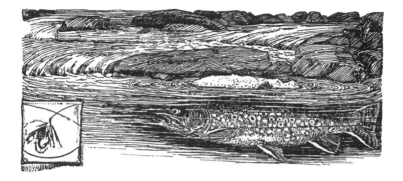

TROUT PROPAGATION.

THE artificial propagation of fishes, that is, taking the eggs, impregnating and hatching them by hand, is reduced practically to an exact science, so far as the eggs of most food-fishes are concerned; and after that the rearing of fry to yearlings or older in the hatcheries is chiefly a matter of cost of food, water supply, and care of the young fish by skilled men. Most fish, too, of all ages are now transported without loss worth mentioning, so the work of actual hatching, rearing, transporting, and planting food-fishes can be planned in advance and carried out as successfully as the rearing of warm-blooded animals. Beyond the point of planting strong young fish in wild waters, the work may be a success or failure, depending upon the conditions existing in the water itself. It may not be an entire success nor an abject failure, but the fish-breeder cannot always foresee which it will be with the certainty that he can foretell the results in his hatchery. Wild waters are always presenting problems to be worked out, to insure the success of fish propagation in them, because the conditions are not always constant in any particular water, and conditions change with different waters. In planting fish in a territory so extensive as is comprised within the boundaries of the State of New York, it is a most difficult matter to determine in advance what conditions exist in all waters that the State is called upon to stock.

Streams that were once natural trout-streams may have become unfit for trout, through lack of shade and the drying up of the fountain-head during a part of the season, caused by lumbering operations. A stream well shaded by forest growth may provide water of a temperature for trout, and when the axe has opened the stream to the sun, the temperature of the water may rise to such a degree that trout cannot live in it. Not one applicant in fifty who asks for trout-fry gives the temperature of the water to be planted with any positiveness. A stream that is a roaring torrent in the spring during the melting of the snows, and is afterward a mere thread of warm water, is not a proper stream for trout of any kind. As a matter of fact, I have seen a brook absolutely dry in the month of August that was planted with trout the preceding May, and probably it was planted in good faith by the person who applied for and obtained the trout from the State.

"*The end of a stiff fight.*"

The State hatches a greater number of fish each succeeding year, but the applications for fish more than
keep pace with the increase, and the applications have
to be sifted and examined carefully that the best results
may be obtained by the Commission in planting fish
only in suitable waters, judging from the information
furnished. If this information is defective or unrelia-
ble or the exact condition existing unknown, the result
of fish-planting may be disappointing.

To show what may be done in the way of stocking
a pond intelligently with trout-fry, Mr. W. C. Witherbee, of Port Henry, obtained 5,000 brook-trout fry
from the State and planted them in a small pond in
Essex County. The pond had once contained trout,
but was so thoroughly fished out that no one thought
of fishing it at the time. It contained an abundance
of fish-food, with a fine inlet stream, spring-fed, and an
ample supply of water. In fact, all the conditions
were favorable, as the result shows. The fry were
planted and allowed to grow for several years, and the
pond was not fished, for there was no boat on it and it
was not generally known that it was restocked. Mr.
and Mrs. Witherbee, concluding that the pond had had
time to recuperate, went there for a day's fishing and
caught five trout, the weights being four and one-half,
four, four, four, and three and three-quarter pounds
respectively, or a total for the five trout of twenty and
one-quarter pounds. The pond was, of course, public
water, and at once it was fished without ceasing. One

trout of over eleven pounds was taken from it, taken,
too, without regard to the ethics of fair angling; and
it is more than suspected that even a larger trout was
taken from the inlet stream at the spawning season, a
trout of thirteen pounds and three ounces. Here are
other conditions to be considered. After a pond is
stocked with fish, and well stocked, water, food, and
temperature all being suitable, what rules can be enforced to insure that the pond will be fished with mod-
eration in season and not at all out of season? But
that is a matter for the lawmakers, game-protectors,
and the consciences of the anglers, rather than for the
fish-breeder; therefore, let us consider a little further
the question of temperature of water suitable for trout.
Waters that already contain trout that do well in them
can be planted, as the fact that trout thrive in them is
prima facie evidence that the waters are suitable for the
fish. In extending the range of trout, or in planting
streams that have been fished out, and in which the
conditions may have changed, it is safe to plant in waters that never exceed a summer temperature of 70° F.
Rainbow and brown trout still thrive in waters of
higher temperature than are suitable for brook trout,
and brook trout will live in well aerated water above
70°; at the same time water of 70.5° has killed both
brook and brown trout, probably because it lacked
vigor, which comes from force and aeration. Trout
grow little, if any, when in water below 40°, and to be
at their best they must have, during a portion of the

year, water that ranges from 62° to 70°, as this temperature hatches the insect life, which constitutes a large part of the food of trout. While food is all-important, trout must have room also, in which to grow. It is self-evident that if trout are planted in numbers to exhaust the food supply, they will not thrive; but aside from that trout must have space to be at their best, for it has been demonstrated that a given number of trout in a certain number of cubic feet of water will do better than the same number of trout in half the quantity of water, both lots of trout being fed the same amount of food.

How far trout may be acclimated to water of higher temperature than that to which they are ordinarily accustomed has not yet been fully demonstrated. In South Africa the brown trout has been hatched in water as high as 79°, and in this country the rainbow have been found to thrive in swift, well-aerated streams that reach 85° F. The experiments of Dr. Davy ("Physiological Researches") to determine the temperature fatal to trout are of interest, and aside from the question of temperature, as they show how trout try to escape when the water becomes too warm. He placed a common European trout (fario), or brown trout of this State, of about a quarter of a pound weight, into a good volume of water at 62°, which was pretty rapidly raised to 75° by additions of warm water, when it became very active and tried to leap out. In an hour the water was increased to 80°, and after a few minutes more to 85°, when it became convulsed, and, although transferred to cool water, died. When the water had sunk to 70° a smaller trout and a minnow were put in, and although the next morning the temperature had sunk to 67°, the trout was dead, but the minnow had not suffered. A par of the salmon, about four inches long, was similarly treated, the water in half an hour being raised from 60° to 70°, and now it tried to escape. The water was raised to 80° and it became torpid and convulsed; at 84° it seemed to have died. A char of about the same size had the water gradually raised to 80°, when it appears to have succumbed. The trout tried to escape by leaping out of the water, while the char kept to the bottom with its head downward, as if seeking for a cooler locality.

The common brook trout of this country (fontinalis) is a char, and undoubtedly acts as did the European char in the experiment, by seeking cooler water downward in a pond when the surface water becomes warm, and searching out spring-holes in streams, so they may be left to their own devices to find the coldest water provided in any stream or pond in which they are planted; but unless the stream or pond contains the cool water for them to find—i. e., below 70°, and 65° would be better—it is useless to attempt to propagate brook trout in it. There are other conditions which operate against the maintenance of trout in a stream. The fish must have gravel in which to make their spawning-beds. Even with gravel but a small percentage of eggs deposited naturally are hatched, but if deposited in the soft bottom they may be lost entirely. During the past season I examined a trout-pond at the request of a committee of gentlemen who had stocked it, and found there was very little gravel where springs boil from the bottom, and trout had been in the habit of spawning, and that little had been covered by vegetable growth. I suggested that spawning-beds be provided by hauling gravel on the ice in winter, spreading it over the places where the springs came from the bottom, and when the ice melted the gravel would settle evenly over the vegetable growth and provide the only thing which appeared to be needed to make the pond suitable for the propagation of trout, for the water was pure and cool, and there was an abundance of fish-food. Streams that are subject to sudden and severe freshets may have not only the spawning-beds ripped up and destroyed, but the food of the fish may be washed out of the stream and will need to be replaced artificially.

Suckers are very destructive of trout-spawn, but after an examination of several small Adirondack lakes, that are natural trout-waters, but from which the trout have become practically exterminated, I am of the opinion that bullheads are to be charged with the destruction, more than any other one thing, men always excepted. Bullheads have not, perhaps, the general reputation for destroying trout-spawn that the sucker enjoys; nevertheless, they are one of the most destructive agents to be found in the water where trout exist.

In the lakes referred to I found that the bullheads fairly swarmed, to the exclusion of all other fish, except a few big trout. They had not only destroyed the trout-spawn, but had destroyed all the food of the trout, and were themselves dwarfed and starved until they were unfit for food. In other waters the bullheads would have sought for food, and fishing would have kept them down, but men, as a rule, do not go into the Adirondack Wilderness to catch bullheads, and consequently all the fishing had been for trout, and the bullheads had multiplied unmolested until they monopolized the water to the exclusion of everything else. In one little lake the bullheads were like a solid carpet of fish suspended in the water under the boat, and with a piece of meat tied to a string about 2,000 were caught in a few hours, as many as seven being lifted into the boat at one time. They were from three to four inches long, and the largest taken was five and one-half inches long, too small to pay for dressing, even had they been fat, which they were not.

On the spawning-beds of lake trout in New Hampshire, bullheads were found so gorged with trout-spawn that they were lying helpless on their sides, and one of the Commissioners who witnessed the sight told me that he was firmly of the opinion that the gorging would have proved fatal to some of the bullheads if the hatchery men had not anticipated the result.

The "Mongaup" at De Bruce.

In waters that do not contain brook trout the bull-head is a most desirable food-fish, and it grows to good size and is always in demand. The waters of the State furnish about 200,000 pounds of bullheads annually, so far as returns have been obtained, more than of any other fish except the shad.

The bullhead is a prolific fish and broods its young, and in trout-waters where it is not sought as food it has only to breed and multiply, barring such casualties as all fish are subject to in a state of nature.

In trout-waters such as I have mentioned, where bullheads have driven the trout to the wall, if fishermen would devote a little time to catching bullheads there would be fewer to devour the spawn of trout and consume their food. There is another remedy for this condition of things, but it is one that can be applied only by the Fisheries, Game, and Forest Commission or its agents.

Every little while it is discovered by someone that trout contain ova in the summer, and there is a demand that the closed season be shortened. The last complaint of this sort that I have noticed was printed in a paper in the northern part of the State. The writer of the complaint found ripe eggs in some trout he caught in August, and he desired that the law should close the fishing on and after August 1st. This gentleman simply made the mistake that others have made, for the eggs were not ripe. If he had examined trout in June or before, he would have found spawn in the females, but it would have been undeveloped ova, the same as he found in August, except that the latter was further advanced. In this State brook trout spawn in October, with some variation, depending upon the water, for the colder the water the earlier they will spawn.

At the Adirondack hatching-station of this Commission, in Franklin County, they begin to spawn about October 1st; at the Caledonia station, in Livingston County, they begin to spawn about October 15th, and eggs are taken as late as the following March, and have been taken as late as April 19th; at Cold Harbor station, on Long Island, they begin to spawn the last of October, but the height of the season is from November 10th to 30th, although a few fish come on in December and as late as January.

In running streams the temperature of the water would follow closely the temperature of the air, and the spawning would be early if the season were cold, except in streams that were largely spring-fed, in which case the temperature of the water would not fall so rapidly and the spawning would be prolonged.

Trout spawn when they are "yearlings," but a yearling is more than twelve months old. All brook-trout eggs are hatched in the spring, and the period of incubation varies with the temperature of the water. The eggs taken the first of October in Northern New York may be 150 days hatching, while the eggs taken on Long Island the last of November will be only about sixty days in hatching. Say that trout are hatched on Long Island in March, during the following summer they will be fry, and in the fall they will be fingerlings, seven or eight months old. The next season they will be yearlings, and as they spawn in the fall of the second season, they will actually be twenty months old at spawning time, although from custom they are called yearlings. Consequently, a yearling brook trout at spawning time is from eighteen to twenty months of age, dating from the time it left the egg. A yearling trout may yield from fifty to 250 eggs, the eggs being one-sixth of an inch in diameter, quite different from the mustard-seed eggs which the fisherman found in the fish he caught during the summer months of the open season. A trout but four inches long has been known to yield forty ripe eggs. Many yearling trout in wild waters are not six inches long, and where the six-inch trout law is observed numbers of trout will spawn before they can be legally killed. If there were no six-inch trout law, it would be possible to kill the trout before they spawned once, and the stock would have to depend almost entirely upon artificial propagation, with but slight aid from natural processes. A "yearling" trout in one of the State rearing-ponds is quite a different fish from a wild trout of the same age, for the State rears yearlings (seventeen months from the egg) that are ten and one-half inches long. Two-year-old trout may yield as many as 500 eggs, and older fish as many as 1,500.

To maintain fair fishing, even in a trout-stream, such work as the State may be able to do in the way of planting the water should be supplemented by all the fish that may come from natural reproduction, and the trout should have every possible opportunity to spawn unmolested.

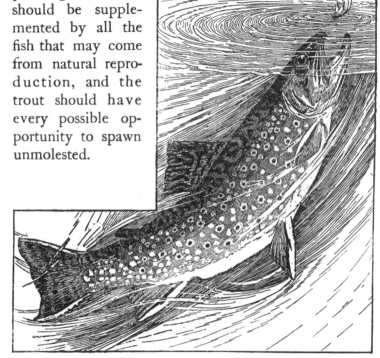

SOME NOTES ON COOKING
BROOK TROUT.

SOME NOTES ON
COOKING BROOK TROUT.

THERE are two ways to test whether a fish is fresh or stale; first, if the eyes are bright and glossy, it is fresh; if sunken, dull, and discolored, it is stale; second, if the finger be pressed on the fleshy part and it is solid and elastic, it is fresh; if the pressure leaves a mark, it is stale. This applies to salt as well as fresh water fish. It has been said that a trout is not fit to eat twenty-four hours after being landed; in that short time the flesh not only loses color, but solidity. No fresh-water fish so quickly changes. Five minutes after death we notice the rich, deep, lovely colors growing paler and duller. In taking a brook trout from the water it will be seen that a thick, slippery, gelatinous substance covers his entire body, particularly the head, shoulders, and tail. When laid on the river-bank in the sun for a few minutes, this substance will cake, and if wet again will moisten as before, but in a few hours, even if it be placed on ice, this jellied substance entirely disappears, leaving the skin thin, soft, and colorless, the flesh insipid, the delicate color gone, and it is in this condition that city people have their trout cooked and served. An angler while feasting his happy and fortunate friends on the trout he brings from his favorite stream, sits and watches them enjoy what he will not touch, for still lingering on his palate is the feast of fresh-caught fish his guide prepared the day before in a clearing of the forest beside a rippling stream.

Many guides prefer to prepare trout (up to ten inches) without being washed, dexterously tearing out the gills, the inside being drawn at the same time, leaving the head, body, tail, and fins intact. For larger trout, the gills should be cut from the lower jaw and back of head, a slit made from the head along the lower body to the fin. On the gills being pulled it will draw the inside away. If done with care, a perfectly clean inside is the result. In all fresh fish the blood is encased in a thin skin close to the backbone, and ought to be pulled entire. A fish so treated can be prepared without the use of water. The case is different if the trout have been carried some distance, the creel at intervals laid down on a sandy beach or covered with grass or ferns and little pine leaves, from the bed of the basket. After being cleaned and prepared, they should then be placed for a few minutes in clear cool water ready for the pan or broiler. Anglers should be careful to thoroughly clean the creel, replacing new ferns or grass every day. It often happens, after long wading, large flies will creep in the basket, and leave fly-blows in the mouth or gills of the trout.

Much depends on the length of time an angler wishes to stay in the woods, and how large his outfit, and also the place he chooses for his camp, the place to build, and method of preparing a fire. An old hand, or guide, can do much even with the primitive two logs, a large stone, with only a small broiler and frying-pan without a handle. Taking for granted that the trout are prepared for cooking and all necessary utensils at hand, the first requisite is a number of square pieces of birch-bark newly cut. Lay the cleaned fish on the inside of the bark, scattering some roasted bread-crumbs or rolled toast mixed with sufficient quantity of salt and pepper, each from small tins kept for the purpose, and the crumbs will adhere to the fish. Then lift them by the head and tail, laying one by one softly into the pan of bubbling fat, either of salt pork, lard, butter, or olive oil. Small brook trout fried quickly in oil, with or without crumbs, is a delicate morsel. If crumbs be fine mixed with a beaten egg, the trout browns and is crisp in a few minutes. To test if thoroughly cooked, place a fork in the flesh. If done, it will sink easily to the bone. Nothing is more distasteful than under-done or unsalted fresh fish. If brook trout are fried with a three-inch slice of good bacon to each fish, the fat is absorbed, and gives the fish a very agreeable taste. When the bacon is partly lean, less salt will be required. But the richest and most delicate dish is to quickly and sharply fry the trout in plenty of good butter, with a bay-leaf dropped in the pan while cooling. The fish cuts up a golden orange, with a decidedly agreeable taste. Even the smell creates a longing for the dinner-bell announcing that it is time to fall to.

In preparing small trout for broiling, two flat stones should be placed to rest the broiler on, and the coals, though hot, should not blaze. Skewer a piece of fat pork or bacon on the top of each trout, and place them on the broiler. The heat will soon melt the fat, partly dripping in a blaze and the rest soaking in the fish. Before turning, take off the fat and skewer it on the other side as before. This will be done easier and better if the broiler is removed from the fire. The outfit is more complete when provided with a bunch of small toothpicks to use as skewers to hold the bacon on and to bind together the opening of large fish. To broil a large fish, it should be cut open along the back, clean by the bone; open carefully and remove the inside. The backbone can be removed by holding the head and shaving the flesh away to the tail. Make small incisions to allow the heat to get through and melt the fat on top. The entire fish is ready to be cooked, the cut-skin side being cooked first, which enables the fat to soak well in the flesh. When

" Ready for cooking."

ready to turn over, lay a clean piece of bark on the top of the fish, lifting the broiler over, leaving the fish on the bark, repeat the turn-over on another piece of bark, and from that bark to the broiler. By that method the fish is properly turned over without breaking. The double or clasp broiler is useless either for small or large fish, as in turning over they slip out on the coals. To bake a two or three pound fish, it should be cleaned, and the tail and fins cut off, the inside stuffed with pork or butter and a small raw onion, and the skin carefully pinned together with small skewers. It is then laid on a dish or Dutch oven. Scatter a little flour mixed with salt and some pieces of bacon arranged along the top with half a cup of water to moisten the fish, which can be basted after the fat melts. In a very hot fire it will cook in forty-five minutes.

Another method is to bake the fish in a hole two feet deep. Build a good hot fire till the charcoal ashes are red. Spread enough green grass or ferns on the ashes and place the fish thereon. Then another layer of ferns. Put on some small dry sticks and let it burn well and build it entirely over with small logs. By the time it is burned through the fish will be baked. This method is not always a success, unless done by an experienced hand, there being no chance to test if the cooking is complete.

A very primitive way to bake a fish is to cover it (undrawn) with clay two inches thick; place it in the hottest part of the fire. The clay hardens almost instantly and the fish in its rough oven bakes through, retaining also its juices. The clay is then poked out of the fire, cooled with a dash of water, and a sharp stroke with a stick separates it from the fish. The skin peels off with the clay and it is ready for serving. If clay is not at hand, wrap the fish evenly in thin buttered tissue-paper and bury this in some wet brown wrapping-paper. Then bake same as the clay. The easiest and quickest way of all to bake a fish is to split, cut off the head, tail, and fins, then season, pin it to a board by wooden pegs, and prop the whole up before a smart fire of hot coals.

To fillet a trout, use a keen, sharp knife, cut off the head and fins, split the back, shave clean along the backbone to the tail, then open the fish flat, and take away the inside. Lift the backbone at the shoulders, and shave the other side. There remains two fillets of boneless fish. Wash in fresh water and dip the fillet in beaten egg and crumbs. Scatter a little fine-chopped parsley and roll up in a ball. Then place a piece of butter on top, and it is ready to bake or fry.

The most sumptuous dish for camp is baked, stuffed trout. This can be accomplished better near a farm or store where materials can be secured. Only a large fish is worthy of being cooked in this manner. Begin by slitting the lower part, take out the gills and inside; wash thoroughly; cut incisions two inches apart along the sides, and skewer pieces of fat bacon in the cuts.

To prepare stuffing, chop separately a piece of suet or fat pork, some sprigs of green parsley, four small onions, the yolk of a hard-boiled egg, and a little dried sage. Take three cups of rolled bread-crumbs, add a few cloves, mix thoroughly together, and moisten with a cup of white wine. Put the stuffing in lightly and skewer the fish securely. Place it carefully in the bake-kettle, pour in half a pint of white wine or hot water to prevent the fish from adhering, lay on the fish some pieces of butter, and place the kettle in the hottest part of the fire. Baste at intervals. It should be cooked in fifty minutes.

To cook fish properly, as in everything else, requires some experience and practice, and a novice should only attempt the simpler methods. More attention should be paid to the proper preparation and cleaning of fish. A work on camp-cooking says: " It is supposed that everybody has known how to clean fish ever since he was a school-boy." A greater mistake was never made. Few men understand properly how to clean and cut up fish; fewer still know how to cut fish served to eat when cooked. A small fish should be slit down the back, the flesh stripped off in one piece from the side. With the left hand, take the head, lift it slowly (a fork holding down the other half), and it will pull along with the backbone the ribs from the flesh, leaving practically two filleted and boneless pieces ready to be eaten. To carve or cut a large fish, it should be first slit down the back, then cut crosswise every two inches, and taken away from the backbone in pieces. When the first half is cut away, disjoint and lay aside the backbone, leaving the head and tail, cutting the lower half as before. Use a keen, sharp knife for cleaning; a dull, broad fish-knife for cutting when cooked. Many guides use their jack-knives and are always slovenly. In preparation for meals, even in camp with few utensils, it is possible to prepare dainty dishes in a dainty way. This can be proved whenever a capable housewife camps and directs the cooking; the results are entirely different. In a thousand ways, everything seems to be more agreeable to a dainty palate. Rough-and-ready methods become habit through constant use of trying to escape extra trouble. Camp-cooking can be just as enjoyable in the preparation as the joys of angling. Hurry, impatience, and loss of good temper take away much from the keen delight and pleasure of camp-life.

ALONG A TROUT-STREAM.

ALONG A TROUT-STREAM.

" It is a spot beyond imagination
Delightful to the heart—where roses bloom
And sparkling fountains murmur ; where the earth
Is gay with many-colored flowers."—FIRDAUSI.

A N ill man is walking down Broadway to his office. Overworked for months, he shrinks from the hard, practical duties of rushing modern business. The half-grown foliage of late May is on the trees in Bowling Green and Battery Park. Robins are calling to each other there. He

167

joys in the fresh wind, and the gulls soaring above North River!

How green the grass is! And there, peeping through, he sees several wild violets, blue as the sky at which they gaze. Presto! the jaded and listless look is gone from the man's face; his heart leaps and hope comes strong and welcome; for before him, summoned by memory, are the violets and the vistas, the thorn-blossoms, robins, pheasants, arbutus, and lilies along the chattering flow of his favorite trout-stream!

Trinity bells are pealing "Rock of Ages"; but the echoes of those peals sing another song to him in his need of rest. It is: "*Only two weeks more! Then you shall be fishing for trout on the little Slagle River!*"

How slowly the fortnight drags by! But a morning comes when, before three o'clock, he is actually wading that stream. At last! Since midnight all the jewels of the skies of June have been shining keenly. It is wild, remote, with even the camp a mile away. He is at the entrance to the Lower Glen. Over the high banks are thickets of thorn-bushes, their wealth of snow-white blossoms filled with dewdrops which have caught and hold the starlight!

Through that sweetest of all earthly things, wild-flower air, comes the far hooting of owls in lonely nocturne. There are whiffs of mint scents, faint smells of fragrant birch and pine-balsam. The slight stir of a sleepy breeze wakes a low whisper in some of the tree-tops, while the stream sings to the sleeping forest, with

> . . . . . " *the still sound*
> *Of falling waters—lulling as the song*
> *Of Indian bees at sunset, when they throng*
> *Around the fragrant Nilica, and deep*
> *In its blue blossoms, hum themselves to sleep.*"

" In the night the great old troutes bite very boldly," said Isaak Walton : so the angler is wading the stream at what the roused camp-cook has called an " unearthly" hour. Far better, he is here to drink in the beauty of the sylvan environment as the mystic hour runs from gold of stars to gold of sunshine.

The stream is wide enough for casting flies without trouble from the white thorn-bushes. Fifty feet below him is a deep pool, just beyond the wraith of foam at the foot of short rapids. Gloom and mystery lie over and in it; he can see the white of foam slowly eddying over its black water under two leaning pines. He moves slowly, then pauses with rubber-clad feet on the white and golden gravel, covered with two feet of rushing water.

Poising the pliable lancewood rod, while the left hand pulls the line from the reel in unison at each pass of the rod back and forth above him, he extends the line with its leader and flies until forty feet of line are in motion. Then, true as bow from arrow, light as down, fluttering as if alive, the White Miller lures go straight to the centre of the pool, and kiss the water.

A flash, gleam, flying spray as a large trout darts from his home under the bank! It is an experience that has often thrilled the real angler. The fish has jumped at and missed the leading fly!

But the next cast is successful. An even fiercer rush, and the angler, with the well-known turn of the wrist on the rod, has the fish hooked! Straight down stream flies the quarry, the reel screaming and the heart of the angler beating hard and fast! A long struggle follows. Almost in the landing-net twice, and yet the trout makes savage rushes for liberty! Soon the prize is secured; joy of possession as a wild, twelve-inch king of the jewelled coat lies on the bed of fern-leaves in the bottom of the trout-creel! For this, and for the gladness of returning health among some of earth's fairest scenes, the angler has journeyed almost 1,000 miles. Already he is mastered by the spell of the remote, wild life, with its mystery and music.

Three beautiful trout are taken from the pool while the starlight dies and the sky grows lighter. Then, startling the ear of earliest dawn, a solitary bird fills the forest with its first note, clear, pure, and thrilling, as if Heaven itself had sent its own winged messenger to herald the coming day! Then another bird takes up the song; then another and another, until all the woods are vocal with melody—now near and joyous, now far and sweet, like " the horns of elf-land faintly blowing."

170

"Tired of the struggle."

"*Skir-reee!*" cries a scared chipmunk as he darts away. A gray squirrel, with tail well cocked, barks and scolds at a safe distance. From far down the stream comes the low drumming of a partridge. Across the bend is a sudden splash, followed by the rattling cry of a kingfisher, who has had his first dive of the day for nothing. A screaming hawk sails away from the dry tree that tops the high bank. "*Up all night?*" inquires a quail.

The hypnotism and delight of it to the man escaped from a busy city office are beyond all expression in words! Blessed hours of recreation!

In the air is the faint odor of smoke, and of boiling coffee. The cook has gone farther down the stream with a heavy lunch-basket, has put six big potatoes before a kindled camp-fire on the brookside, and then has caught five larger trout from a deeper pool; breakfast there is nearly ready. The roasted potatoes are done to a turn—how well the cook can prepare them! And out from the little frying-pan come the five trout, swimming a half hour ago, and now garnished with tender water-cress from that bank of it close at hand. Abundant coffee, cream, toast, butter! The breakfast is served on two snowy napkins spread over a mossy knoll; the dishes are pieces of freshly cut birch bark, the seat is a birch log. Peerless dining-room—a June sky curved in azure benediction above a wild pine-forest filled with sough of the wind through its aisles—with bird-notes, with the voice (so glad!) of the soul of the wilderness—the talking stream whose rapids reflect the early sunlight down one of the long aisles, and cause it to dance on the foliage. Not all the chefs and banquets in the cities of the round world could produce such a meal as this, with such a breakfast-chamber!

For the wealth of beauty is everywhere. Laurel and rhododendron blossoms are around him — wild lilies, trailing arbutus, and white strawberry blossoms! Finally, the forest rises above a blue carpet of violets. How the angler loves them! He stops the cook from plucking them for a boutonnière. He almost wishes, as he lies beside a thick cluster of their blooms, that he might strike hands and feet in the kind earth, take root himself beside his favorite flowers, and nevermore abandon the happy companionship. The little, nodding, blue comrades! He feels that they are sentient— know and are grateful for his love and insight. He is charmed by their wild, shy life. As he lies prone and drinks from the spring below the bank, one of them takes advantage of a sudden gust of wind to actually nod *at him* several times!

" *It is just a little violet on the bank above the spring ;*
  Just a little point of blue that nods before the saucy air :
And as he notes the beauty of the wee and winsome thing,
  He feels that it is glad to see him back and drinking there."

And now comes proof that the angler sees and knows the beauty of his environment. For he is not fishing. He could talk for hours of rods, lines, leaders, and reels—of camping, guides, tents, pack-horses, canoes; of the various flies to be used according to season, location, lights, hours of day or night, on a dozen widely separated streams. He has fished on the Peribonca in Quebec, the best salmon-streams in Newfoundland, the far-famed Nepigon, and the fierce waters of a dozen rivers in British Columbia that are guarded by black mountains whose bases were green with foliage; while their peaks, sometimes two miles high, carried snow-banners in every high wind. He knows Pennsylvania's best trout-streams; and the waters of the Muskoka Region; besides the Au Sable, Shuswap, Two Medicine and St. Mary's Lakes in Montana, and Square and the Sourdnahonk Lakes in Maine. Trout from the Margaree in Cape Breton, from the Tabusintac and Bartibog Rivers in New Brunswick, and the Morell Stream on Prince Edward Island, have been brought to his creel by hundreds. The best cruising for edible salt-water fishes—that around Albemarle and Pamlico Sounds—is familiar to him. But *nowhere else* exist such wildness, remoteness, wealth of sylvan enchantment, such flavor to trout, such health and life in air and water, such music in a stream, as along the peerless little Slagle River!

He is realizing this, and is happy to the point of fear. He could easily fill his creel with trout; yet he does not cast the flies. For he is in a hypnotized state. He will not even light his morning cigar; its smoke would pollute the air of a place which has " become religion." And he would sooner take a drink of whiskey before St. Peter, the ancient fisherman who now guards the gates of Paradise, than here, right in a Paradise upon earth.

The rod is laid on the half-submerged log where he sits, with his rubber-clad feet in the water. He really hears and sees!

What a contrast to the scenes he beheld last summer along Granite Creek, which flows into the head of St. George's Pond in Newfoundland! There, the hillsides were yellow with ripe bake-apple berries; barrens were gray with Arctic moss; caribou grazed in plain sight on many hills. Moose-birds, tame by reason of their ignorance of human presence, roosted on the ends of the little logs on the camp-fire before the tripod tent. Marsh-hens called and fluttered; and at night, from far above, could be heard the quacking of ducks and the thrilling "*honk! honk! honk!*" of the stout-hearted old wild ganders, each winging his way toward Labrador at the head of invisible wedges of night-flying geese. Great trout were in the pools of that stream; and the steel-gray color of its gravelly bed was very beautiful. And yet, even among such scenes, the angler had longed for the music, the flower and bird life, foliage and mystery of the Slagle! Its waters flow around his legs now! And they seem to talk to him as they rush:

" Where have you been, my devotee ?
Why have you roamed so far from me ?
Thrice welcome back to my fair shore !
Now learn to love me more and more."

He sees the flash of the body of a brook trout as he leaps from the brook, in pursuit of a butterfly, wandering too near the water's surface for safety. The line and flies have drifted from the log. Flash! a trout strikes one of the lures, pulls the rod into the stream, and the owner scrambles after it. Now he is casting again, and filling the creel. Nearly every effort brings some response. In pools, behind rocks, on the ripples, here by the bank, there beneath those logs, yonder in the foam of the rapids, and in places where least suspected, glittering in beauty, crimson-spotted, always ready for a bait, lurk and play the wild brook trout. The wild trout is the ideal fish, the fish of the poets and the sportsman, who often feels that the breeding-pond is the half-way house to a fish-stall in a market.

And so he wanders down the brook, happy, filling his hours with best recreation. Steeper, higher, wilder, in lordly, many-colored scenes, grow the banks of the Glen. Great trout lie in the waters which eddy, rush, and glance in silvery wilfulness over an intaglio of white and golden gravel that beautifies the swift current.

Thus, all too quickly, passes the angler's day. The

late afternoon light is over all as he again stops, and looks, and listens.

To his right is a high knoll, mottled with moss-growths, its base sandalled with the white star-points of wild strawberry blooms, and the tiny pale-blue flowers of forget-me-nots. Beyond, is the brown, far-spreading carpet of the forest, splashed by blue of violets, white of lilies, yellow of daffodils! The whole left bank is a mass of dark wintergreen growth, edged at the water with mint and cress. Yonder is a little slope exquisite with the pale pink flowers of the anemone. Buds of wild honeysuckle are opening down there on the little island. Blossoms of laurel, rhododendron, trailing arbutus! Forest odors, bird-notes, whispering stream, murmuring foliage! Mottled patches of sunlight and shadow dance under the great trees where, last night, the strident calls of the whippoorwills were ringing. A mother partridge is trying to coax her brood of chicks across that log over the stream! Beautiful! No wonder the gray-haired angler loves it all. " The infinite Night with her solemn aspects, Day, and the sweet approach of Even and Morn, are full of meaning for him. He loves the green Earth with her streams and forests, her flowery leas and eternal skies—loves her with a sort of passion in all her vicissitudes of light and shade: his spirit revels in her grandeur and charms—expands like the breeze over wood and lawn, over glade and dingle, stealing and giving odors. Nature is to him no longer

176

an insensate assemblage of colors and perfumes, but a mysterious Presence with which he communes in un-utterable sympathies."

So this angler looks, listens, and feels more and more.

Every water-curve is full of grace, fantasy, and ease of motion, like a wind-swayed flag. And he studies the currents, full of color, clearness, mantlings of shad-ows, prismatic lights running over the white gravel of the bed, or darting through the foam-fire. And at still pauses is as much in the water as above it—boughs, foliage, blue sky, drifting clouds, all softened and etherealized by reflection.

> " *Sweet views which in our world above*
> *Can never well be seen,*
> *Are imaged by the water's love*
> *Of this fair forest green.*
> *And all is interfused beneath*
> *With an Elysian glow ;*
> *An atmosphere without a breath,—*
> *A softer day below.*"

This effect is heightened by the music of the water-flow. Old anglers have ears trained to nicest sense of sound in the music of running water, and will know the physical conditions, even when unseen, which cause many of the notes of sound in a trout-brook.

The impact of the hurrying water on the air causes vibrations that determine the notes of the liquid oboe.

When deflected from a bank in mass, the water has the swishing sound of swift volume—crisp and full of life. Confined and made rapid in a little cañon or cut, its tone is deepened and becomes sonorous.

Or it falls over a half-buried timber and deepens to a low roar, which is slashed with purling dots of sound as drops fall singly into the current. From underneath this shell of swift water come echoes of partly drowned notes from the back-current below, and purls from roots and boughs around which the turned stream hurries. Gurgles ensue—the compressed air below varying in density with the varying volume of the water-leaps, the tones of the back-flow struggling through, with the whisper of air intermingled as it comes from the breaking bubbles with which the boiling pool is brightly opaque.

Or a fallen tree with its hundreds of boughs and twigs forms obstructive points of sounding current—tiny, but the whole furnishing a low, droning complaint. All these notes are varied by the width of stream, volume, depth, speed, angles of obstruction, character of the bed, kind, amount, and density of foliage, incline and height of banks, changes in echoes and resonance being endless, and even being affected by the dryness or humidity of the air, and the mingling of foliage sounds as winds are light or strong.

"*A pool where big fellows lie low.*"

Up the stream is a broad shallow where the brook flows over partly submerged rocks, spread evenly, with a slumberous sound, like a steady wind moving through thick woods. Falling over the even edge of a wide dam the water has much the same sound. Unobstructed on inclines, rapidly flowing water in small volume has the inimitable purl, so exquisite that even in music the sweetest sounds are called liquid, like a tinkling rill. And the notes that blend from different water-tones are always in concord, never in dissonance. Flowing under many conditions, meeting multiform obstacles over even a single rod of its course, these notes combine and make a certain "tone" or pitch of musical sound. Put a log across the brook, choke it with rocks, or remove those already there, and all the minor sounds are changed—also the general tone and pitch of the water-music. Or the stream will part with some portion of its water volume, which will run into still nooks and limpidly go to sleep.

Thus the tone, volume, and blended orchestral effects of the water along a rushing trout-stream are endless in variety and beauty—but all perfect. And the feeling of the hearing, sensitive student will be played upon until some echo of that music will be roused in his own spirit as he studies it all in its light and gloom, sunshine and shadow, storm and peace. So in all ages the best poets have studied and sung of the sound of flowing water, and have peopled their musical brooks with singing nymphs and wraiths of water-sprites.

Wild life, hypnotism, the home of Health! The true angler sees much, but will realize that as compared with what is about him, he sees very little.

Pluck a single leaf and look at it carefully. Even a skilled artist must keep it before him as a model, to mimic the delicate veinings and exact shape. Break a bough from a maple-tree, and try to see it. Some of the leaves are mere lines to the sight—edgewise; others are foreshortened; many are shaded by companions. Through them reigns an intensity of reflection and brilliant semi-transparence acting upon and through surfaces extremely complex in shape, curve, and relative position. The light is in among the leaves and alters the appearance of the bough from within as well as without. Turn it, hold it in any position, and it is perfect; yet not another bough in all these miles of forest is just like it! Multiply the woods until they are a wilderness swayed by wind or quiet in unity of rest—flecked by driving cloud-shadows or flooded with moonlight or sunshine. Manifestly, we cannot see them. Only a few of even the subtle and weird patterns woven by ferns and mosses, and flowering grasses and plants, on the floor of the forest can be noted or understood.

Above all, Mystery reigns. The stream drowses under long, partly seen roofs of foliage, or under loving, interlacing boughs of a water-tunnel whose portals and winding sides are a tapestry of leaf and twig, misty with rain, unearthly as they shine in the wan smile of dying sunlight; even more real and divine in ghostly semi-darkness at night! Opaline lights play through still lagoons in deep glades where the twin sisters of Silence and Twilight keep noonday watch, and "all the cheated hours sing vespers." Foliage melting away in distance to mystery of banks and masses, softest shadows deepening into black gloom, lonely stretches of the stream covered with Nature-Glory in their remote windings! Yet over each small section of such a scene is the mystery of color, form, interlaced shade. Here is what a man of sharpest sight has said of it :

" *The stones and gravel of the banks catch green reflections from the boughs above. The bushes receive grays and yellows from the ground. Every hair-breadth of polished surface gives back a little bit of blue of the sky or gold of sun. This local color is again disguised and modified by the hue of the light, or quenched in the gray of the shadows.*"

But over and in all reigns the deeper Mystery of Life. Visible forms and their beauty are not the strongest attractions of the trout-stream. Grant that mystery of soft depth of gloom, grace of motion in water, and of greatest delicacy of color are before the angler. What enchantment is there in even all this lovely environment to create such fierce longing for it, such content when possessed? Blue sky-fire may burn like a steadfast sapphire through emerald foliage; the pride of fern-plumes may wave and rustle in their green refreshment,—gold and pearl may throb in clouds whose shadows wing their way over mountain, glen, and forest,—all through a sun-shafted fantasia of gold-dusted wine-air which is perfumed by arbutus, lily, violet, and forget-me-not,—the blossoming life all in a tangle of fragrant day-dreams. Fairy tints may dance and quiver through that baby of prismatic mist, the tiny rainbow as it spans the cascade. All the glamour and riot of wild freshness may dwell in the mysterious woods, waters, sky, as a June breeze makes the whole a harp of whispering leaves, purling crystal, and curving blue. Place the angler in closest touch with it all, as he wades the stream with ears, heart, and spirit receptive and alert,—foliage near, rushing water about him, changing, intermingling light and shadow over him as it falls in dancing fretwork. Yet even all this does not explain his great love. What causes it?

It is because in this Nature about him is a Mystery of Life. An evasive, sleeplessly unwearied living principle dwells in the leaf he may pluck and crush, and is forming its colors, shaping its forms. Fern and flower, traced with life-streaming veins, specially textured, with hues that blend and part again, substantially present, possessed, yet hold a secret of living being and growing life that forever eludes his search, and always will. Life even more mystic than the spirit that he feels in himself is present before him, inscrutable, regnant, locked and barred away from his knowledge.

Thus for him Nature wears a double aspect—that of substantial presence and infinite remoteness. She dominates him with love of possession and of unattainable desire. He looks with mortal eyes upon her material features; yet he may gaze forever upon the veil that hides her invisible secret of life, and she is yet Isis—a Magnet of Mystery. Therefore he kneels, a rapt, glad, and humble devotee, before the closed gates, the thin wall beyond which are the secrets of her vivifying existence. Besides, she stands, like himself, between an Eternity of the Past and one of the Future, seeming to call and beckon from a fathomless Abyss whose depths his eyes will never pierce. She is fairest of the fair in visible forms; yet in her mystery of life she is unseen and unapproachable even in closest communion. So he loves her with unutterable love.

But he knows all is benign, and the vital import of the power that has created. But how, and by what facts and mysteries of life? No answer comes. He will not fathom the secrets; but he will realize more and more the divine wisdom in making so much unknown as all is borne forward. He will be sure that it is inconceivable that all is not of holy import and being—sure that all the mystery is blessed. Half-read messages and tones of sphere-music will come to him as he wonders at the Earth, and at himself, standing there with her, both between two Eternities. And thus his faith is satisfied, and his love is crowned!

The result is inevitable. With bowed and reverent head the angler hopes that when he has crossed the Delectable Mountains, and, one poor thread in the web of universal history, has waved back his mute farewells to his favorite trout-stream before he enters the Unknown and is swallowed by Oblivion, a merciful and loving Heaven may furnish to him the counterpart of this brook. Will he not find a heavenly stream on that Other Side? Will not its waters sing as with a new song, its forests whisper, its flowers enchant? Yes, for there stands the message of Holy Writ, the last words of John, Seer and Prophet—words of inspiration and promise: "And he shewed me a pure river of water of life."

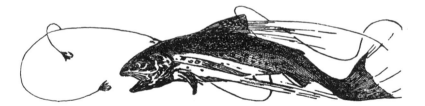